Dress, Gender and Cultural Change

Dress, Body, Culture

Series Editor **Joanne B. Eicher,** *Regents' Professor, University of Minnesota*

Advisory Board:

Ruth Barnes, *Ashmolean Museum, University of Oxford*
Helen Callaway, *CCCRW, University of Oxford*
James Hall, *University of Illinois at Chicago*
Beatrice Medicine, *California State University, Northridge*
Ted Polhemus, *Curator, "Street Style" Exhibition, Victoria & Albert Museum*
Griselda Pollock, *University of Leeds*
Valerie Steele, *The Museum at the Fashion Institute of Technology*
Lou Taylor, *University of Brighton*
John Wright, *University of Minnesota*

Books in this provocative series seek to articulate the connections between culture and dress which is defined here in its broadest possible sense as any modification or supplement to the body. Interdisciplinary in approach, the series highlights the dialogue between identity and dress, cosmetics, coiffure, and body alterations as manifested in practices as varied as plastic surgery, tattooing, and ritual scarification. The series aims, in particular, to analyze the meaning of dress in relation to popular culture and gender issues and will include works grounded in anthropology, sociology, history, art history, literature, and folklore.

ISSN: 1360-466X

Previously published titles in the Series

Helen Bradley Foster, *"New Raiments of Self": African American Clothing in the Antebellum South*
Claudine Griggs, *S/he: Changing Sex and Changing Clothes*
Michaele Thurgood Haynes, *Dressing Up Debutantes: Pageantry and Glitz in Texas*
Anne Brydon and Sandra Niesson, *Consuming Fashion: Adorning the Transnational Body*
Dani Cavallaro and Alexandra Warwick, *Fashioning the Frame: Boundaries, Dress and the Body*
Judith Perani and Norma H. Wolff, *Cloth, Dress and Art Patronage in Africa*
Linda B. Arthur, *Religion, Dress and the Body*
Paul Jobling, *Fashion Spreads: Word and Image in Fashion Photography*
Fadwa El-Guindi, *Veil: Modesty, Privacy and Resistance*
Thomas S. Abler, *Hinterland Warriors and Military Dress: European Empires and Exotic Uniforms*
Linda Welters, *Folk Dress in Europe and Anatolia: Beliefs about Protection and Fertility*
Kim K.P. Johnson and Sharron J. Lennon, *Appearance and Power*
Barbara Burman, *The Culture of Sewing*

DRESS, BODY, CULTURE

Dress, Gender and Cultural Change

Asian American and African American Rites of Passage

Annette Lynch

Oxford • New York

First published in 1999 by
Berg
Editorial offices:
150 Cowley Road, Oxford, OX4 1JJ, UK
70 Washington Square South, New York, NY 10012, USA

Berg is an imprint of Oxford International Publishers Ltd.

Library of Congress Cataloging-in-Publication Data
A catalogue record for this book is available from the Library of Congress.

British Library Cataloguing-in-Publication Data
A catalogue record for this book is available from the British Library.

ISBN   1 85973 974 1 (Cloth)
          1 85973 979 2 (Paper)

Typeset by JS Typesetting, Wellingborough, Northants.
Printed in the United Kingdom by Biddles Ltd, Guildford and King's Lynn.

For Mitchell D. Strauss,
my faithful and patient husband,
colleague, and companion.

Contents

Acknowledgements

This manuscript was enhanced by the editorial contributions of the members of the editorial board for this series, most significantly Joanne B. Eicher and John Wright. I would also like to recognize the insight and suggestions of my blind reviewer in the formulation and development of the African American chapters. The support of Kathryn Earle also helped to move this volume from concept to completion.

Thanks is also due to the Hmong Americans and African Americans who shared their community, rituals, and thoughts with me. Tiffany Jackson, my research assistant on the debutante material, was a great help. I greatly enjoyed my fieldwork in both communities and feel that my life as well as the lives of my daughters were expanded by our experiences.

Finally, special special thanks to my family for their support and encouragement. Recognition is due to my husband, Mitchell; my daughters, Mary and Madeleine; and my parents, Alma and Lewis for their patience and faith in my work. Also, a big thank you to Parker for being a good baby and letting his mother finish her book.

List of Illustrations

1

Introduction

This book explores and analyses how young men and women in two American cultural groups negotiate and instigate changing gender constructions by the dress[1] and appearance styles they wear during adolescent rites of passage to adulthood. The two populations, Hmong Americans and African Americans, have vested interests in transforming and/or reconstructing gender as a means of more effectively and successfully negotiating positions of power and influence in American society. Coming-of-age rituals in both communities provide arenas of negotiation wherein young people dress to assume adult roles in their communities and in so doing both challenge as well as reinforce history and tradition through their appearance styles.

The Hmong are originally a Chinese ethnic group that fled to Laos escaping discrimination in the first two decades of the nineteenth century. Their presence in the United States is relatively recent. Beginning in the middle of the 1970s they entered America as refugees from the Vietnam War and were given some degree of economic and social assistance by the government. As of February 1991, the Minnesota State Refugee Office unofficial estimate of Hmong living in Minnesota was approximately 21,000 with 95 per cent living within the St Paul/Minneapolis metropolitan area. This is the highest concentration of urban Hmong Americans outside of California which has the largest overall population in the United States.

Hmong American refugees in St Paul, similar to nineteenth-century immigrants, are primarily (92 per cent) rural people attempting to assimilate into an urban industrial center. In addition to this settlement problem, 72 per cent of Hmong refugees were not able to read or write in their native language when they first entered the United States (Mallinson, Donnelly, and Hang 1988: 21), therefore learning to read and write in English was a greater challenge compared to most cultural groups relocating to America. Michael Baizerman's and Glenn Hendrick's (1988) study of Southeast Asian youth in

1. Dress is defined as 'an assemblage of body modifications and supplements displayed by a person in the presentations of self' (Eicher & Roach Higgins 1992). The supplements include clothing and jewelry. Dress will be used as an all-encompassing term, and clothing where specifically applicable.

the community in which I worked points out the special difficulties that confront Hmong American youth because of high welfare dependency rates compared to other Southeast Asian American populations in the area. They argue that self-sufficiency is difficult for Hmong youth to envision or achieve because they are being raised in families where welfare is an integrated part of daily life. The 63 per cent Hmong welfare rate compares with figures of 38.2 for the Lao, 31.0 for the Vietnamese, 41.2 for Cambodians, and a 5.5 per cent rate for the general population in the area (1988: 38).

The African American community I worked in was settled in the early twentieth century. Blacks were first recruited into the area in order to break a railroad strike in 1911. The blacks that migrated to the area came primarily from the South and had minimal education. Most were males, and most moved to the area specifically to find good jobs (Lane 1972). The second major migration of blacks from the South to this city occurred during and after World War II. Between 1950 and 1960 the African American population in Waterloo nearly doubled. In a state with a small population of blacks, Waterloo became the urban center with the highest concentration of African Americans in the state (Lane 1972). Similar to the St Paul/Minneapolis Hmong American community, the Waterloo African American community is in the Midwestern United States. It is a smaller community of about 9,000 within a total urban population of approximately 125,000. While the Hmong American community is one of the largest and influential in the United States, the black community in Waterloo is small and relatively isolated from American centers of black culture.

However, trends affecting African Americans throughout the United States have also been felt in this community. The number of middle-class blacks holding professional or management positions in the United States has risen dramatically since the 1950s. In 1950 10 per cent of employed blacks could be considered middle class with professional management, or sales positions (Gates and West 1996: 9). The ranks of the black middle class have grown substantially to the point that one-third of all blacks are now considered middle class, with 20 per cent of employed African Americans now working in professional or management positions (Gates and West 1996: 19). Taken as a single decade, black middle class in America doubled in the 1980s, primarily as a result of affirmative action hiring practices (Gates and West 1996: xi). The percentage of blacks attending college has also increased substantially, with figures of 3 per cent in 1960, one in ten in 1970, and one in three in 1996 (Gates and West 1996: 19). This optimistic picture is complicated however by a growing division between African American middle class and the growing numbers of blacks living in poverty. Currently one-third of all African American families are living in poverty and one-half of black men between 25 and 34 do not have a job, or are underemployed (Gates and West 1996: 24).

Rites of Passage to Adulthood

The public celebration of New Year, the fieldwork focus of the Hmong American analysis, is a two-day event held over the Thanksgiving weekend in a large civic center in St Paul. In the United States, as the community and individuals struggle to make sense of change and integrate into social and economic structures, gender roles have become points of conflict between men and women and between older and younger generations. The New Year celebration and the rites of passage rituals enacted during this time help young people and adults reconcile traditional gender roles with the new gender roles emerging in the United States.

The Debutante Cotillion Ball and the Beautillion Ball in the African American community are held in the spring as a celebration of the accomplishments of graduating seniors of promise. They are sponsored by men's and women's professional organizations with a commitment toward supporting the growth and development of future leaders within the community in terms of mentoring and recognition. They are a part of larger national efforts on the part of the black middle class to use their resources for the betterment and growth of the community through social actions directed toward youth and young adults.

In contrast to the refugee status of Hmong Americans, African Americans were forcibly removed from their homelands and entered the United Status classified as owned property. Importing of West African slaves to America occurred between 1619 and 1808, therefore African Americans have endured 300 years of discrimination on American soil. As an American cultural group with a long history of compromised identity, young men and women in this community reconstruct themselves in part as a response to the stereotypes of black female and male identity that emerged as a result of slavery and discrimination in the past.[2]

2. Numerous published accounts discussing dimensions of the stereotypes and discrimination of Africans Americans resulting from slavery and colonization are available. Recommended are Fausto-Sterling 1995; Gaines 1996; Gilman 1985; Jewell 1993; Mercer and Julien 1988; Pieterse 1992; Schiebinger 1993; and Wiegman 1995.

Body, Dress, and Gender Construction: An Overview

Scholarship on dress and identity has long posed a convincing argument that attitudes and habits of dressing and otherwise modifying the body are slowly absorbed throughout the socialization process. Gregory Stone's influential and early (1965) theoretical work on developmental aspects of dress and social identity analyzed dress-up behavior of children as an experimental phase in which different identities are tested against the reviews of a significant audience, most often other family members and parents. Stone argued that a child's identity is formed in part as a response to the response he or she receives from others. Normative appearances are most often expressed as individuals strive to fit into their social and cultural context and thus dress to receive positive reviews of their dress from others.

Gender is one of the first identities that human beings acquire, first through investiture and then through socialization. Even at birth, parents assign different adjectives to male versus female children. Research done on American infants (Rubin, Provenzano, and Lunea 1974) has shown that opposite sexed but otherwise matched infants are viewed differently by their parents within 24 hours of birth. Boys are typically described as strong, hardy, and well coordinated. Girls are more frequently described as little, cute, and soft. These babies then tend to be dressed by their care givers to conform to culture-specific gender expectations. In America, boys tend to be dressed in outfits making references to active definitions of self, such as sports; and girls more often are dressed to solicit positive comments on their appearance, a more passive form of self-identity.

The second stage of primary socialization as outlined by Stone (1965) is the play stage. During this stage pre-school children experiment with and test different gender identities on their surrounding audience of family members, friends and care givers. Work on symbolic interaction and development indicates that children rely heavily on outside reviews of their appearance in the formation of gendered identity. Children learn normative standards of appearance and behavior by monitoring and responding to the reactions of others to their dress styles and actions. These reactions coupled with gender images they absorb through mass media help the child formulate a gender identity which fits socio-cultural expectations.

In adolescence males and females begin to dress to express multiple identities and to express principles and value structures. While dress is used to rebel against some aspects of socialization, gender identity, as a part of primary socialization, is typically not seriously challenged. Despite the feminist movement, even political versed American adolescent girls still tend to use dress to attract, then to use that attractive ability as a source of power. Recent

Coding of Gender Ideology: "Doing" versus "Being" (An Artificial Dichotomy)

Doing	Being
Emphasis on achievement and action	Emphasis on appearance and attraction
Physical effectiveness	Physical attractiveness
Adventure script in popular media	Romance script in popular media
Agonic (aggressive and active) power	Hedonic (indirect and attracting) power
Ideology of building character	Ideology of maintaining character ("placed on a pedestal")

Figure 1.1 Susan Kaiser's (1997) gender role dichotomy.

research on college-age female populations in the United States (Holland and Eisenhart 1990) confirmed the continuing influence of this gender construction on young women in the United States. In contrast male success continues to rely more heavily on active as well as attractive abilities. As a result, their dress styles tend to express physical and intellectual competence, rather than simply attractive ability. Susan Kaiser's (1997) gender role dichotomy (see Figure 1.1) captures typically Euro-American models of gendered appearance and behavior.

The tendency of people to grow up and self-train themselves to fit within political and cultural systems that underlie prevailing gender constructions has been used by feminists to argue that racism and sexism is perpetrated not so much through coercion as voluntary self-compliance. As put forward by Michel Foucault and quoted by Susan Bordo, 'There is no need for arms, physical violence, material constraints. Just a gaze. An inspecting gaze, a gaze which each individual under its weight will end by interiorising to the point that he is his own overseer, each individual thus exercising this surveillance over, and against himself' (Bordo 1993: 27). Thus responsibility for the continuation of unfair distribution of wealth and power between men and women rests in part in the court of those being oppressed. By dressing to fulfill a passive role, by conforming to expectations by focusing on their attractive ability, women often unconsciously support the system they are battling to change. While individuals battle for change, bodies and by extension dress often conform to existing expectations; so, as the inner voice argues for change, the dressed body remains locked into the existing social order (Diamond and Quinby 1988).

In contrast to those examining the role of dress in reinforcing structural patterns of oppression, my research examines how dress and appearance are used within rituals as a means of gaining agency and control for the wearer. As argued by Bordo and Foucault, I have found in many cases that everyday dress and appearance often reinforces existing power structures. However, within ritual display dress often challenges existing structures and initiates a process of transformation and reconstruction.

Research on male gender constructions has most typically taken as a point of departure the concept of hegemonic masculinity. According to Robert Connell (1995) there is always a version of masculinity that is held up as most successful. It is, in his words, 'the culturally exalted' version of masculinity. The hegemonic ideal of masculinity is dynamic, argues Connell, but it is always linked in some way to institutional power. Marginalized masculinity, according to Connell, is a male gender construction of a subordinate group that is cast in relationship to the hegemonic ideal.[3] From this vantage point the business suit symbolizes hegemonic masculinity and linkages to institutional power structures. In contrast gang styles are expressions of marginalized masculinity worn by young men attempting to set up alternative systems of validity as a result of exclusion from hegemonic positions of control and power.

Following the thinking of Kobena Mercer (1990) I prefer the term 'counter-hegemonic' to marginalized masculinity. Mercer uses counter-hegemonic to describe gender constructions that force or move toward recentering processes. The advantage of this term is that it implies the possibility of structures that challenge and change dominating normative values. This term fits my research better as I found, particularly in the case of the African American material, that counter-hegemonic trends started by the black community were picked up by hegemonic models of masculinity, thus the counter becomes the mainstream in some cases of cultural interchange.

The Concept of Ethnicity

The question of what to label the dress worn by the young African and Hmong Americans is not an easy one to answer. There is much debate concerning what labels to use for dress associated with distinct cultural groups (see Baizerman, Eicher and Cerney 1993; Eicher 1995). In an important sense the struggle for appropriate terminology is political. When we accept a classification system we inherit a way of dividing up and thinking about the world. The classification system for dress outside of the Euro-American fashion mainstream, including such categories as primitive dress, tribal dress,

---

3. Connell (1995) points out that while males from marginalized sectors of American culture, black athletes for example, may serve as models of hegemonic ideals, their personal success has no trickle-down effect on others within the cultural group.

tribal markings, and folk dress implies an ethnocentric system with roots in the colonial era. While not blatantly stated, the words carry inferences that Euro-American dress is more civilized, that progress is from the primitive other to the civilized us, and that we have the right to label the cultural products of others. Similar to the problems related to the term marginal masculinity discussed earlier, many of the accepted categorizing systems for dress assume that white Euro-American culture is the center, and everything else is in the margins. This is problematic for numerous reasons, not the least of which is that the division between Euro-American style and other cultures is becoming artificial as influences spread back and forth over cultural boundary lines. Finding the 'center' that influences all else becomes problematic as the reality of cross-cultural exchange becomes recognized and accepted.

The concept of ethnicity (and its associated term ethnic dress) are at the heart of the struggle, in part, because ethnic has been used as a convenient substitute for less politically correct terms such as tribal and primitive (see Chapman, McDonald and Tonkin 1989: 14). Because of this convenience, ethnicity is a slippery concept that has been used in many different ways by many different scholars (ibid:17; Roosens 1989: 19). The term ethnicity began to be commonly used in the field of anthropology in the 1960s and 1970s (see for example Barth 1969; Cohen 1973; Epstein 1978; Glazer and Moynihan 1975; Moerman 1964). With the organization of nation states from formerly colonized areas the ethnic group became commonly used to refer to smaller groups within nation states. About this time the idea of the American melting pot was being challenged. As American anthropologists stayed home to study cultural differences ethnicity became a key concept. The term thus emerged in response to the need for a label for the persistent expression of cultural difference in the modern nation state. It was generally used to refer to the self-conscious marking of difference by a cultural group within and in opposition to the majority group within a nation state (Roosens 1989).

Two general approaches to ethnicity dominate the research literature: (1) structuralists and (2) culturalists. The structural approach takes the lead from Frederick Barth's (1969) influential collection of essays emphasizing the importance of ethnic boundaries. In contrast, culturalists argue that an ethnic group is defined on the basis of its cultural characteristics. Structuralists emphasize the instrumental aspects of ethnicity and their work often illustrates how ethnic boundaries are manipulated in order to gain political or social power (e.g. Cohen 1973; Schildkrout 1974). Typical of this approach is Joan Vincent's comparison of ethnicity to a tool, 'Ethnicity in operation is, like all else social, a tool in the hands of men; it is not a mystic force in itself . . . there are times, perhaps numerous, when it lies in no one's interest to admit ethnic distinctions into social and political encounters. Ethnicity is a mask of confrontation' (1974: 10). Vincent stresses the elective quality of ethnicity. The idea that it can be used to accomplish goals and objectives in the same sense as other forms of social identity.

In contrast culturalists argue ethnic groups share common history, values, attitudes and beliefs. Nina Glick-Schiller and Georges Fouron point out that this approach is problematic in that cultural variation often exists within a bounded ethnic group (1990: 331). Instead they propose an ideological approach to ethnicity that argues for tentative and variable correspondence between ethnic group boundaries and cultural differentiation. The ideological approach posits that by *believing* in the idea of ethnicity groups simultaneously resist and accommodate to domination and exploitation (Glick-Schiller and Fouron 1990: 332).

Jonathan Sarna (1978), working specifically on the American immigrant experience, uses the ideological approach in this interpretation of emerging American ethnic groups. He points out that American ethnic groups enter the United States identifying themselves by region, village, or family but are labeled and treated as an ethnic group by American institutions and power structures. He goes on to argue that ethnic groups use cultural content, including dress, to construct symbols of cohesiveness and pride as a defensive response to discrimination. Thus fragmented immigrant groups become cohesive ethnic groups by accepting and eventually symbolizing externally drawn ethnic boundary lines. This particular approach, because of its emphasis on symbolic expression of ethnicity is useful to scholars working with dress as an expression of group identity.

John Comaroff posits that the process of marking group boundaries is 'basic to human existence' (1987: 306). Similarly, Howard (1990) argues that ethnicity is 'an instance of the human propensity to categorize experience according to sameness and difference' (259). Howard uses this stance when he states that 'ethnicity ought not to be looked at as a distinctive phenomenon' (259) and that the concept has much in common with 'conceptualizations of kinship, community, friendship, and other types of social relatedness'. In contrast with Howard, Comaroff calls for a conceptually distinct definition of ethnicity and focuses attention upon the fact that the substance underlying boundary lines between groups varies with changes in social and cultural circumstances.

Two basic distinctions Comaroff draws are between what he labels *totemic* boundary lines and *ethnic* boundary lines. *Totemic* boundary lines are established between equally powerful and structurally similar groups. The groups divided by totemic boundary lines share much cultural content, but maintain some degree of distinct identity. Totemic dress styles, for example, might be used to mark differing village subgroups within a larger ethnic or national setting. In contrast, *ethnic* boundaries are asymmetrical power-based relationships between structurally dissimilar groups. Central to Comaroff's definition of ethnicity is the idea that ethnic consciousness is 'the product of historical processes which structure relationships of inequality between discrete social entities' (ibid: 308). Using this definition, ethnic dress styles thus emerge when small, less powerful groups are posed in relationship to larger politically dominating groups. For example, one might argue that native American ethnic dress styles based upon historical prototypes continue to be worn in festival settings because of the structured inequality that exists in their relationship with dominant American culture.

Within this volume I use the term 'ethnic' when I refer to Hmong American New Year's dress because at this historical juncture it is being worn to mark a boundary line between the Hmong as newly settled American refugees and mainstream elements of American culture. In contrast, aesthetic influences evident in black style have infused American expressive culture to such an extent that to refer to black dress as 'ethnic' and posed in relationship to a separate American fashion mainstream is not appropriate. Currently, among some elements of American youth, black style not only influences but constitutes the fashion mainstream. The term 'ethnic' is thus used carefully within this volume and is confined to discussions of Hmong American dress as an expression of newly emergent ethnic identity.

Theoretical Approaches to Ritual

Rites of passage into adulthood are used by all cultures as a means of transmitting and reinforcing political and cultural norms regarding gender roles specific to distinct ethnic groups. Dress as a visible expression is often a vehicle used to express normative expectations for men and women. Jean Hamilton and John Hamilton's (1989) ethnographic research among the Karen in Thailand documents and analyzes the symbolic importance of dress in the transmission of gender:

Thus 'things', material artifacts, in this case, dress can have a powerful influence on the socialization of individuals and the continuance of a cultural system. For Karen women, married women's dress is critical for the culturally appropriate psychological state of a woman, for the continuity of the matrilineal tradition of cultural transmission, and for our understanding of the cultural system. (20)

Likewise, Catherine Daly's (1987) work among the Kalabari of Nigeria analyzes and documents dress worn to indicate different stages of the female life cycle. With each successive stage the dressed woman is further adorned in symbols of cultural commitment related to assuming the expected gender roles of a fully mature Kalabari woman.

These studies illustrating how dress worn within ritual reinforces existing gender constructions fit within a more general approach to the study of culture, with goals of discovering essential and stable aspects of society through analysis of cultural celebrations such as initiations and funerals. Recent analysis of ritual has recognized that while a significant role of ritual is to restate or visibly display essential guiding principles of a cultural group, it is also the arena wherein culture is transformed or reconstructed to fit changing social, economic and political realities. This approach to ritual holds that culture is both transmitted and transformed during the course of a celebration. Participants make culture their own by taking the cultural guidelines of the past and reinterpreting them to fit and guide their lives. So, to use a common example, while wedding ceremonies most certainly function to reinforce and restate culturally normative behavior, they are also an arena that focuses attention on changing aspects of everyday life. Changing vows, ritual actions, and dress have historically expressed and helped to transform relationships between married couples, relationships of the bride to her parents, and notions of appropriate gender roles for both men and women.

The effects of varying engagement or commitment of those individuals who participate in rituals has been debated and discussed. The question is asked, 'How can you argue that ritual transforms everyday life, if all participants, or at least a majority of participants, do not express whole-hearted commitment to the ritual enactment?' Sherry Ortner (1978) working on rituals among the Sherpa, took the stance that while reasons for attending a ritual celebration may vary from deeply felt commitment to simply 'nothing else to do', all participants ultimately became engaged in the action, and were therefore transformed by the process. In my work I interpret the participants' willingness to dress for the event as a visible display of commitment. I argue that those who dress for a ritual performance are moved to meaningful participation through the process of dressing to fit the prescribed or changing roles within the celebration. In my judgment the act of taking the effort to dress appropriately for a culturally significant event is a physical and mental act that draws the participant into the theatre, the performance, and the discourse on culture which *is* ritual.

Two theoretical models of how ritual helps initiate change inform my work: Clifford Geertz's concept of ritual as both a model of and model for reality and Victor Turner's interpretation of ritual as a formative as well as reflective performance. The contribution of Geertz dates to an influential essay titled 'Religion as a Cultural System' first published in an edited volume in 1966 and later in a compilation of essays in 1973 (Geertz, 1973). Turner's (1988) work on ritual and performance is the culmination of a lifetime of fieldwork yielding dynamic interpretations of culture that contrasted vividly with the then typical static, functional, and structural models in text books.

Geertz specifically addresses cultural aspects of religious life in his essay, but his ideas concerning ritual are useful in a broader cultural context. He defines ritual as 'an historically transmitted pattern of meanings embodied in symbols, a system of inherited conceptions expressed in symbolic form by means of which men [and women] communicate, perpetuate, and develop their knowledge about and attitude toward life' (1973: 89). I expand Geertz's work to include dress as a form of symbolic behavior and, as such, a cultural pattern that expresses, transmits, and helps create cultural attitudes and stereotypes concerning appropriate male and female gender roles.

Using religion as an example, Geertz argues that the power of ritual is to fuse cultural *models of* everyday reality with *models for* transcendent or idealized reality. As individuals participate in ritual Geertz argues that the symbols that fuse the two models transform the participants by helping them imagine or experience transcendent or transformed versions of everyday life. Thus meaning is infused into daily experience through the power of ritual. What startles and transforms the participants is the juxtaposition of the idealized and the normative occurring as symbols drawn from both everyday life and ritual crossover and reflect on each other. In the words of Geertz, 'In a ritual, the world as lived and the world as imagined, fused under the agency of a single set of symbolic forms [including in my work dress], turns out to be the same world' (1973: 112). The coming together of the real and ideal in a single set of symbols is what creates transformation and heightened consciousness.

From the perspective of cultural construction and transformation of gender through dress, what happens within ritual is the meeting of real and idealized/ or imagined conceptions of gender roles as expressed through dress and related behavior. Participants draw from a range of available dress options to create symbolic ensembles that function as visual references to actual or hoped for gender identities and roles. The comparison of normal everyday gender-based expectations with idealized roles made visible through dress results in self-conscious examination of normative habits and roles. Resulting debates concerning appropriate dress reveal underlying attitudes toward female and male gender roles as made manifest through appearance.

The second major contribution to the interpretations of ritual posed in this book comes from the life work of Victor Turner. Turner spent much of his academic career exploring the role of ritual in expressing and resolving cultural conflict. Richard Schechner summarizes Turner's contributions by stressing that he viewed ritual as a performance that is 'inherently dramatic because participants not only do things they try to show others what they are doing or have done' (1977: 120–3). Schechner stresses that Turner saw ritual as a means of changing social position or role. In Schechner's words, 'For Turner . . . the basic human plot is the same: someone begins to move to a new place in the social order; this move is accomplished through ritual' (1977: 120–3). The above quotes are central to understanding how I use Turner's ideas to interpret the formative role of dress in the cultural construction of gender within this volume. In both the Hmong American and African American case studies adolescent males and females attempt to overcome social and economic obstacles and move to a new position in American society. Rituals, in this case coming-of-age ceremonies, are used as arenas to present, debate, and establish new versions of gendered identity.

The ritual celebrations examined in this volume are all classic rites of passage into adulthood. Typical of rituals at this stage of life, participants are dressed (or dress themselves) and are presented to fit and fulfill adult roles in the sponsoring society. The social crisis underlying each of the case studies focuses on the felt-need of these young people to define themselves, in contrast with being defined by history and/or tradition. Both case studies are similar in that they focus on an American sub-cultural group; they differ in that Hmong Americans are recently relocated refugees while African Americans have a long history of interaction with American culture.

Everyday life, with its unconscious practices and behaviors is thus posed in contrast to the conscious performance of ritual. On the one hand, daily life, and with it normative dress patterns, tends to reinforce existing attitudes, cultural systems and political structures. Dress worn within ritual, on the other hand, can reinforce the present, pay testimony to the past, or attempt to change toward the future. When we have an 'excuse to dress', such as dressing for a ritual experience, we consciously create an image of ourselves, rather than dressing to fit an existing normative role in society. We have the power to dress the way we would like to be perceived, rather than the way we are customarily perceived. We can dress to fit the normative ideal, or dress to challenge it.

As previously stated, many times the image created for ritual fits or is an idealized version of expected cultural norms, and therefore makes the participant feel accepted and committed to fulfilling normative roles. This form of ritualized dress reinforces historically linked identities. However, as supported by Turner's work, rituals are also arenas wherein we dress to challenge and explore social and cultural expectations. In the case studies in this book,

Americans from two cultural groups use dress to transform and redefine normative gender roles. African Americans, who have a history in which black identity has been used as a justification for constructing compromised images of both male and female gender, use dress worn within rites of passage to adulthood to reconstruct positive and capable images of themselves. In contrast, Hmong American adolescents use dress worn within ritual to challenge historical gender constructions and negotiate newly emergent versions of normative male and female gender roles more respondent to the demands of their new lives in the United States.

The intersection of gender and race within the case studies allows exploration of how the young adults and their sponsoring families and community leaders use dress to negotiate the relationship between gender and cultural identity. Having a formal excuse to dress provides these African American and Hmong American teenagers with an opportunity to explore, challenge and transform themselves both as men and women and as members of cultural groups with distinct histories and bodies of aesthetic expression.

I have provided a background chapter for the Hmong case study as they are a relatively new American ethnic group and many readers may not be familiar with their culture and history. African American history and culture has been extensively researched. I have chosen not to attempt to summarize available published work but rather I have used notes when appropriate to guide the reader to additional readings in select relevant areas.

2

Hmong American Dress and Culture: An Overview

To study a language is to study a way of dividing up the world. The things we choose to name, and the relationships we draw between one named category and another, structure our interactions with each other and our physical and metaphysical world. The symbolic weight granted dress and cloth within the interpretations posed here may in part be justified by the linguistic tie in the Hmong language between creation of a civilized space by cultivation of land and the creation of a human being by dressing the body.[1] *Ncaws* means to clear or hoe the ground; when prefaced with *khaub* (meaning to wind around, encircle, wrap) it is the word for clothing. Significantly, the term for clothing changes to *khaub hlab* when one speaks of old clothing or ragged clothing, thus reserving the term *khaub ncaw* for civilized and presentable dress.

Paj ntaub is the general term used to refer to all the varied textile arts created by Hmong women. Again, the Hmong language connects cloth to the earth: *paj ntaub* means 'flower cloth.' Techniques used in this art form include embroidery, appliqué, reverse appliqué and batik as well as the additive arts of assemblage. These arts like other *kev cai* (customs) discussed by Nicholas Tapp (1988) are self-consciously practiced by Hmong Americans as they use the customs of the past to fashion a meaningful life in diaspora.

My research reveals that dress helps to formulate new parameters of civilized behavior for Hmong Americans in the United States. As the community struggles to define appropriate male and female behavior dress functions as a means of expressing shared and conflicting views in how gender should be constructed in the American context. In particular, my research focused on the contribution of traditional and American dress styles to transmission and transformation of male and female gender in the United States.

1. Similar linguistic ties between words used in reference to the dressed body and civilized space are noted by Sylvia Boone (1986) among the Mende and Robert Thompson (1973) among the Yoruba.

Fieldwork Methods

I began my research with exploratory and informal interaction in the Hmong American community. While I had observed Hmong Americans and their hand work at the local farmer's markets, my first contact with the Hmong American community was made when my family sponsored a Hmong family immigrating from a refugee camp in Thailand in December of 1987. The family was composed of a married couple in their early twenties, two female children (pre-school age), and an elderly aunt. Our initial contact with this family eventually led to contact with an extended family including an older and younger brother and their families.

My status as a married woman in her early thirties with two young pre-school-age children gave me a certain degree of natural entree into this extended family. The advantage of being perceived as a mother of children and wife in a community where the family is valued is stressed by Warren (1988: 14–15) in her discussion on the impact of gender on fieldwork experiences. She points out that an individual is afforded a certain degree of internal viability when his or her social status meets basic cultural expectations grading gender roles in the targeted fieldwork community. In the Hmong American community in which I did my work, it was assumed that both men and women would marry and have children. While I was considered normal, a single unmarried woman in her early thirties may have been assigned a more marginal status. Our Hmong American male married friends were delighted when they found out that I was five years younger than my husband, as most Hmong men tend to marry younger women. The implication was that we had done it right, because we had done it their way. They were pleased by the fact we fit their expectations and therefore fit into their world.

On-going informal contact with the three families over a period of three years provided a valuable portrait of the resettlement of an extended Hmong American refugee family. Each of the three families experienced resettlement in slightly different ways providing a broader understanding of the problems and issues confronting Hmong Americans. In particular, as my research turned toward teenage Hmong Americans, contact with the younger brother and his wife provided keys to understanding high school and gender relationships from the vantage point of youth. Throughout the duration of my research, I consciously attempted to keep interaction with these families as natural as possible. As a result, I was able to compare information gathered in more formal and systematic situations with information absorbed in a more casual and real context.

Following the recommendations of Margeret Eisenhart and Dorothy

Holland[2] (1983) and Donna Eder and Stephen Parker (1987), I conducted more systematic fieldwork in social situations that would allow me to observe and document interaction among peers. Fieldwork included tutoring Hmong students in high school classrooms and in their homes, interviews conducted at sports events and in private homes, a weekend camping trip with high school Hmong American culture clubs as well as extensive fieldwork at four annual New Year celebrations in the late 1980s and early 1990s. The New Year was chosen as a research focus because of its central place in the life of teenagers in the community and its continuing role in courtship. It is also one of the few social events that young women as well as young men are allowed to attend. While teenage males often attend other school-sponsored events, young women most often do not have the same freedom to socialize. The courtship focus of the event, the importance of dress, and the popularity of the event with a large number of young men and women in the community made it a rich means of gaining an understanding of the role of dress in reconstruction of male and female gender in the American context. In the following section of this chapter I will provide the background information on Lao Hmong dress styles related to the dress I observed at the New Year.

Dress in Lao Hmong Society

Different Hmong dress styles were historically associated with different regions of Laos and Thailand and with different linguistic sub-groups. The clearest distinctions existed between the two broad categories of Green and White Hmong dress, which in turn corresponded to the two major linguistic sub-groups. The following two chapters will provide more description of dress styles for men and women in these two sub-groups. In general, Green Hmong handwork can be most simply identified by the use of blue batik to produce pattern. White Hmong handwork used the reverse appliqué technique to produce intricate white patterns.

Scholars trace the roots of the Lao Hmong sub-groups which are marked by corresponding differences in dress styles to China where the Han Chinese ascribed separate status to various sub-categories of Miao (Geddes 1976; Dewhurst and MacDowell 1983; Cubbs 1986). Sub-styles of dress in the

2. Research by Eisenhart and Holland (1983) on the cultural transmission of gender in the American context indicates that peer groups play a significant role in reproducing gendered attitudes and behaviors. Eder and Parker (1987), also working within the United States, conducted ethnographic research examining the effect of school-sponsored athletic events on cultural transmission of gender. They argue persuasively for the movement of gender transmission research from formal school settings into real social situations.

Lao context were internally perceived and understood categories. Sally Peterson (1990) points out the extensive information that was carried by dress in Lao Hmong communities:

> the individual is recognized as Hmong by other Hmong, who with a glance will know if the stranger they meet shares their dialect, marriage customs, house style, spiritual offerings, standards of beauty in clothing and song, and other cultural facets that distinguish one subgroup from another. They mutually recognize, in a twinkling, what kinds of limits might structure their future relationship. (118)

Dress thus immediately set up a relationship between the Hmong individual wearing the dress and the Hmong individual perceiving the dress. The two individuals knew how to respond socially to one another and what relationships were possible based upon internally understood visual cues.

Lao Hmong dress marked what John Comaroff (1987) would call a totemic boundary between the related sub-groups. The bounded groups were structurally similar and had roughly the same amount of power. The sub-groups of Lao Hmong spoke different versions of the same language and tended to perform rituals in slightly different ways. These cultural differences, while internally perceived, were often not externally appreciated. Dress as a visible sign was more often noticed and commented upon by outsiders, thus perhaps accounting for the use of dress by the outside world to label the differing sub-groups.

Hmong style dress, worn in the Lao hills on an everyday basis, is reserved in America for special occasions. Hmong American women are typically married in Hmong style dress and families dress in these styles for family photographs in the summer. The largest public display of Hmong dress styles in the United States is the annual public celebration of the New Year which in St Paul is held over the Thanksgiving weekend. The ritual presentation of men and women of marriageable age takes place within the context of the ball-toss courtship ritual played as a part of the New Year celebration. The remainder of this chapter will provide historical and ethnographic background material on Hmong culture and describe historical and contemporary versions of the New Year celebration.

Historical Background

Miao vs. Hmong

There is debate centered on the historical ethnic borderlines surrounding the Miao people of China but scholars agree that the Hmong were once classified as part of this questionably defined group. Some scholars skirt the problem and imply that Miao (a derogatory word meaning barbarian or savage) is an externally ascribed name for Hmong and the Miao are the Hmong and the Hmong are the Miao (see for example Quincy 1988). Most however acknowledge the classification problems which emerge from the fact that Miao has been used to refer to various groups throughout Chinese history.

Drawing from research conducted on site in China in 1982, Schein (1986: 77) points out that in the first half of the twentieth century, seventy to eighty sub-groups were classified under the common designation Miao. Intensive efforts to identify and classify China's ethnic minority populations began in 1949 (Schein 1986: 74). Ethnic group members divided themselves into over 400 separate minority groups. Beginning in 1953 Chinese ethnologists used comparisons between language, religion, customs and dress styles to lump similar ethnic groups together resulting in an official count of 55 'minority nationalities,' as they are referred to by the Chinese (Schein 1986: 75).

Largely on the basis of linguistic evidence, the self-identified Miao, unlike some of the other ethnic groups who were later reclassified by Chinese ethnologists, were left an intact ethnic group in the official count of minority nationalities. Termed 'coethnics' the range of cultural diversity within the commonly designated Chinese Miao population is wide. Despite the marked cultural differences between the Miao sub-groups, Schein states that group identity, based upon the common minority designation Miao, is growing and the subgroup names are rarely used except as an internal means of identification. In the field Schein found that the Miao are beginning to present themselves by subgroup only when specifically prompted (1986: 77).

The name Miao originally carried derogatory connotations. It was an externally ascribed name which the self-proclaimed 'civilized' Han Chinese used to refer to what they considered the uncivilized and savage minority populations they were attempting to dominate. Peterson (1990) points out that Father Savina, writing about the Hmong in 1924, makes the first written reference to the fact that the people called Miao by the Han Chinese referred to themselves as 'Hmong,' a word in their own language meaning man. Despite this early preference for an internally generated and more positive identifier the Chinese Miao are both officially classified and self-identified by the once derogatory name. Schein argues that there is 'significant evidence that the negative connotations [associated with the name Miao] have indeed been dispelled' (1986: 77).

In contrast, the Hmong who fled China as a result of discrimination based upon the ethnic classification of Miao, such as the Lao Hmong, tend to resent the use of the term. Unlike the Chinese Miao they have not gone through a reinterpretation process resulting in a more positive feeling for the once derogatory name. Dr Yang Dao[3] (1982), a leading Hmong American intellectual and economist who was formerly a refugee from Laos, came out in support for the ethnic group name Hmong in 1975. Hmong is translated by Yang Dao as 'free man.' Alternatives to the ethnic group name Hmong, such as Miao or in later form Meo, are considered racial slurs by many Hmong Americans. Many Hmong Americans are aware of the linguistic roots of Miao which imply less than human status and barbaric behavior and resent the fact that at one point in their history outsiders referred to them by this name.

Hmong Migrations

The Laotian refugees that now call themselves Hmong Americans migrated out of south and southwest China into the mountains of Southeast Asia in the early part of the nineteenth century. Dr Yang Dao gives the ten-year decade of 1810 to 1820 for the Hmong arrival in Laos (1982: 6). In Laos Hmong lived in small villages at high elevations. They practiced the technique of slash and burn agriculture and grew a variety of crops for both human and animal consumption. Rice was the staple food in the Lao Hmong diet supplemented by some meat and vegetables. Corn was grown to feed the chickens, pigs and horses. Opium poppies were grown for internal medicinal use as well as for a cash crop. Cash raised from the sale of opium was used to pay taxes imposed by the French, to buy tools and sewing materials, and to send children to school. Prior to the disruption and massive casualties from the Lao Hmong involvement in the Vietnam war, Dr Yang Dao estimates that the Lao Hmong population rose to approximately 300,000 (1982: 3).

The Vietnam War and its Aftermath

Laotian Hmong were slowly drawn into the Vietnam conflict. Beginning in 1945 they began, for humanitarian reasons, to help French soldiers hiding in the mountains from Japanese patrols. When the battle against the French presence in Indochina was taken over by the North Vietnamese, the Hmong who had helped the French were targeted for elimination. In response, the Hmong sided with the French and were thus inadvertently drawn into a modern war. After the withdrawal of the French in 1954, the Hmong continued to fight for the freedom of their country. Beginning in 1961, the Lao Hmong were drawn into a twenty-year secret war directed by the American Central Intelligence Agency (see Robbins 1987 for an American

3. References in the bibliography are listed under the family name Yang. Hmong customarily reverse the order of personal and family names.

pilot's account). Official Hmong casualty figures were estimated at 18,000 as of 1969 (Dommen 1971). Following the collapse of the Royal Laotian Government in 1975, loyalist Hmong were forced to flee to Thailand to escape persecution under the hands of the Laotian communists.

General Vang Pao and 3,000 of his soldiers led the retreat as they fled from Vientiane, Laos to Thailand in May of 1975 (Tapp 1988). From May to August of 1975 as many as 25,000 Hmong refugees fled Laos and crossed the Mekong River into Thailand (Tapp 1988). An additional 24,000 Lao Hmong refugees entered Thailand in 1979. When Nicholas Tapp did his fieldwork in the Thai refugee camps in the 1980s, there were 46,000 Hmong housed in five separate camps (1988). Relocation to Western countries resulted in approximate Hmong populations (as of 1992) of 13,000 in France, 650 in Australia, 650 in Canada, and the staggering figure of 120,000 in the United States (Yang 1993).

Ethnographic Background

Family Structure

The Hmong as people are subdivided into clans that trace their origin to a common ancestor. There are fourteen to fifteen common clans (Vang 1979). Marriages within the clan are not permitted. A woman moves into her husband's clan when she marries and the children produced by that union are considered members of the husband's clan. Within each clan the Hmong are further subdivided into large extended families who trace their lineage back to a common known ancestor (Greenburg 1987). The extended family, translated as *peg neeg* (literally meaning helping group), is an individual's social economic support structure. Families tend to work together as a group and decisions affecting individual members of the group are often debated and decided by leaders within the family. Individual Hmong feel responsible for the well-being of not only their immediate household family members but everyone within the extended family.

Individual families composed of a man and one or more wives lived in extended patrilocal households headed by a single male elder (Bishop 1984). The authority of elder members of the household was highly regarded. Male children tended to marry and raise their children in their parents' house until the death of their father. At this juncture the household typically divided beginning the cycle once again. The surviving parent generally lived with the youngest male child until his/her death. Young women thus became a part of a new lineage when they married and left their family of origin.

Death rates for children in Laos were high. This fact, paired with the strong cultural value placed upon large families, led to a high birth rate and possibly the acceptability of polygyny. Social organization was based on clan membership which in turn determined patterns of courtship and marriage.

Religion

A majority of Lao Hmong practiced a religion emanating out of three inter-related elements: animism, ancestor worship and shamanism (Dunnigan 1982). The spirit world consisted of three sets of spirits: the spirits (*dab nyeg*) of the civilized world inhabited tame spaces such as villages, cultivated fields and homes; the spirits of the bush (*dub qus*) inhabited the wild untamed world surrounding Hmong settlements; and the ancestor spirits (*dab txwvkoob*) who have the power to intervene in behalf of their descendants (Scott 1987). Illness and misfortune, in the Hmong religious world, were caused by the loss of the human soul (*plig*) to the spirit world or the possession of the human body by a spirit. The shaman (*txiv neeb*) mediated between the world of the spirits and the human world. Shamans could be male or female and performed a range of ritual acts focused upon the retrieval of lost souls, the purging of possessed human beings or the satisfying of the ancestors.

Lao Hmong New Year

The most important ritual event of the calendar year was the annual New Year celebration. Hmong New Year celebrated in the Lao village context, as described by Hmong American elders, was a three- to five-day annual holiday celebrated at the close of a busy agricultural season (Vang 1990). It was an opportunity for families and friends to gather together and renew the bonds tying the community and family together. Clan leaders and shamans performed rituals of renewal ushering in the New Year, banishing the cares of the old year, and making peace with the spirit world in order to safeguard the community for the coming year.

The holiday as recalled by the elders was a time of courtship and marriage. The busy agricultural year allowed little opportunity for parents and potential lovers to meet and arrange marriages. The New Year, as a time of celebration and community, brought families and young people from differing clans together to eat, to perform rituals, and to play games. A central feature of the New Year was the playing of a courtship ball-toss game which was accompanied by the singing of poetry. As the paired youth played ball and sang, relationships were formed many of which resulted in marriage. I quote the following from an interview with a Hmong American elder:

The Hmong work very hard on their farms – Saturdays, Sundays it didn't matter. They never had a holiday during the year, but at the twelve month's end, we made 30 kinds of food to celebrate once a year. We worked so hard at the farm we didn't have time to go to other villages to see who might be good marriage partners for our sons and daughters. Then the elders would make 30 kinds of food to celebrate the holiday, and the youth would have a chance to come and join in and select one another. During the New Year many young men and women fell in love and got married. (Vang 1990)

The New Year was also a time of spiritual renewal. George Scott (1987) underscores this function of the New Year in his description of the meaning of the New Year drawing from the ethnographic accounts of William Geddes (1976) and Hugo Bernatizik (1970):

Of the various farming-related ceremonies in the Hmong annual Lunar cycle, the New Year Celebration (*naj peb caug*) was the most elaborate and important. It began on the first day of the new moon in the 12 month, which coincided with the end of the paddy harvest, and lasted from four to seven days. At this time all work would cease, the linage members who had established satellite farming campus would return to the main village to begin preparations for the celebration. Standing as a spiritual and material marker between the old year and the new, the ceremony was aimed in general at removing the evil influences that had assimilated during the previous year and ensuring an adequate supply of good fortune for the next. All the specific rituals performed during the celebration involved expiation, supplication, and sacrifice intended to reassemble the ancestral souls and familiar spirits back at the village to secure their spiritual assistance for the coming year. (37)

The need for the elders to perform ceremonies calling back the families' souls to the village was expressed in the interviews with elder Hmong Americans:

The year was brand new. The family members' souls had to play a long way off and they forgot to come back home, so we used chickens and eggs to call them back home. Then my family members will stay healthy. If you do not call the souls back home, then your family members may get sick. Our children hope that they will get an egg on New Year's Day. The souls have the same hope, too. That's why Hmong people called their family members' souls every year. (Vang 1990)

The idea that the New Year is a time for renewal is further emphasized by the building of a passageway through which all members of the family pass from the old into the new year. Evil is left behind as individuals pass through the opening and good is returned to the heart. A male Hmong American elder explained the construction of the passageway and its meaning:

So, in the year end you must go to the West or the sunset and cut one tall thin tree and bring it home. Then you cut some bamboo leaves, and tie them together and make one long string. You tie one end to the top of the tree and one end to the bottom of the tree. All the head of the households must use bamboo leaves to sweep all the evil out of your home and bring the bamboo leaves to the arena where the tall tree was. Then the old man stood up at the bottom of the tree with a rooster and all the people went under the tree and their string. You must go nine rounds only. Five rounds mean that you sent all the evil away with the sun when it sets. Four rounds come back, mean you send all back – things away – that can take you to the evil, and you should get some good things by heart to come back to you . . . after you send all the evil away, then you come back home and cut the paper money and put it on all your doors in your home. When the evil comes back, it has no way to go through your home and your family will stay healthy all the year round. (Vang 1990)

The Role of Dress and Cloth in Lao Hmong New Year

Women sewed throughout the year to prepare new clothing to be worn first for the New Year celebration and subsequently through the year for everyday attire. Treasured and costly clothing not worn on a daily basis was taken out of the storage baskets to add additional pomp to the newly sewn ensembles. Because of the central importance of the courtship ball-toss ritual young unmarried men and women were adorned in all their New Year finery. Female beauty was judged not only by biological attributes but by the quality of the handwork worn on the body, so girls and their mothers worked hard to create fine New Year ensembles. Families' ability to provide New Year finery for their family members was a symbol of strength, industriousness, and well-being for both men and women.

The interviews I conducted using a hand-sewn story cloth[4] depicting the passageway ritual revealed some differences in the symbolic weight given to cloth within the performance depending upon clan membership. As depicted on the story cloth some but not all clans symbolically marked the passage from the old to the new year by hanging woven bundles of the past year's clothing from a rope stretched between two trees (see donut shape hanging from the rope in Figure 2.1). As the family walked through the passage between the trees, cares and troubles of the past year were symbolically left behind in the woven bundles of clothing suspended above their heads. A teenager described the making and meaning of bundles in this way, 'Every

---

4. Story Cloths were made by the Hmong while they were in refugee camps in Thailand and typically depicted rites and memories that the Hmong did not want to forget. They were typically drawn by men and executed by women.

Figure 2.1. Story cloth depicting the New Year passageway ritual. Photograph by Lynch.

person's clothes in the clan, we tear a little bit from him and a little bit of clothing from everyone and we tie it together. And it means all those bad things should stay here and not with those people' (AL-M-03).[5] The bundles, like the New Year celebration more generally, underscored the fundamental value placed upon family relationships. Representative clothing from individuals was collected and it is then woven together into a bundle representing the family.

The New Year celebration and its rituals were carried by the Hmong into the United States. The public as well as private celebrations have become an important means for expressing collective identity and for passing traditions from the older to the younger generation. The next section of this chapter will describe the private and public celebrations as they are practiced in the United States, with specific attention paid to the role of dress in the rituals and festivities.

5. Information from my interview data is referenced by my initials and my subject's gender and interview number.

Hmong American New Year

Ethnic festivals modeled upon the past but in revitalized form have been a part of American life since the early large European migrations of the nineteenth century. Celebrations similar to the Hmong American New Year were staged by many nineteenth-century American immigrant groups. John Bodnar's (1987) study of these festivals points out that within the festival format many cultural expressions of the past were transformed by the new immigrant groups to reflect upon and make sense of their new American experiences:

> Almost no dimension of the traditional life immigrants knew remained unaffected by the new order which confronted them. At the same time most newcomers did not hesitate to exploit or draw upon past belief and practice if it is some way would facilitate and render intelligible their new life and condition. Even though most newcomers were unskilled toilers, they were in a sense almost all craftsmen in their ability to creatively fashion culture and meaning to suit their daily social and psychological needs ... Folk culture was simultaneously transformed and revitalized in urban America, as immigrants sought to enter capitalist society on their own terms and formulate their own definition of their status and condition. (1987: 185)

Victor Turner's work on ritual supports Bodnar's claim that ethnic festivals turned tradition to the end of making sense of the present. By using rituals as a means of revitalization and transformation, new immigrants' lives were made more meaningful and manageable through linkages to the past. By using the ritual context to embed new problems in old rituals immigrants were able to work through their new experiences and make sense of them. In a similar sense Hmong Americans have reinterpreted the traditional New Year to fit its new American context.

In the Hmong American community in St Paul, the New Year is celebrated both privately within family homes and publicly in a large civic centre. In contrast with New Year celebrations of the past, both private and public New Year celebrations in the United States are rituals in which conflict related to change and relocation is negotiated. Most of the teenagers I interviewed as a part of my fieldwork participated in some versions of the New Year rituals within their own homes. Descriptions of the privately performed rituals ranged from fairly simple celebrations focused on sharing a meal to larger, more complex celebrations led by an elder male member of the family. The most elaborate home celebrations included the building of a modified version of the passageway described earlier in this chapter and the making of cloth bundles from pieces of dress worn over the past year.

Teenagers were careful to point out that the dress used to make the bundles in the United States is American-style, not Hmong-style dress. When asked why, one teenager replied that the clothing pieces collected and tied together must be from garments worn regularly over the past year, 'It must be a T shirt or something – something I have worn a lot that has the good and the bad in it' (AL-M-05). In other words it must be a piece of cloth that has absorbed the experiences of the wearer during the past year. A second male teenager stated it in this way, 'They [must be] old clothes that have stayed with your body a long time' (AL-M-03). Pieces of American-style dress thus carry the contemporary experiences of Hmong American youth into a ritual rooted in the past that is led and best understood by Hmong elders. The elders, as the ritual leaders and creators of the cloth bundles, actively translate American life and clothing into the Hmong idiom. They help the Hmong American community make sense of the present by using cloth as a bridge between life as it was lived in Laos and life as it is now experienced in the United States.

The private celebration is an attempted bow to the past in terms of honoring elders and religious traditions. A small number of teenagers described very formal efforts at the private celebration to show respect to elder members of the family. One interviewed teenager put it this way, 'During the time of the New Year we have a ritual that we pay respect directly to him [the oldest male member of the family]. All the people are younger than him, we go to his place and we pay respect to him by kneeling down and he gives us a New Year blessing' (AL-M-05). More typically, the teenager's descriptions revealed underlying conflicts between the older and younger generations that were either struggled with or temporarily resolved within the home-based ritual. Some teenagers commented that many of their peers no longer formally or informally honor the elders as a part of the New Year celebration. Some admitted that they rarely attend the private celebration rituals. Instead, they use the opportunity to socialize with teenage relatives gathered together into one household for the holiday. Others said that they were uncomfortable with the old rituals because they were Christian now and feel that the old religion is old-fashioned and not meaningful.

The public celebration of Hmong New Year in St Paul, like comparable nineteenth-century ethnic celebrations discussed by John Bodnar (1987), draws on long-standing practices, but adapts to its new American context. Although Hmong of all ages attend, the celebration is focused primarily on youth. The public New Year brings together old and new aspects of Hmong life in a juxtaposition of ancient ritual and American popular culture. The auditorium is dominated by young people engaged in the traditional ball-toss courtship ritual during the day and dancing to live Hmong rock and roll in the evening. Middle-aged and elderly Hmong Americans watch from the balcony and from the sidelines, but Hmong American youth dominate a majority of the main floor and stage activities.

The stage shows generally begin in mid-morning with dramatic reproductions of the New Year rituals as they were privately practices in Laos. When queried from the audience, teenagers tend to say that they are performed so that the young people will know what it was like in Laos. Most people in the audience appear to watch rather than participate in the rituals, although small crowds gather in front of the stage as the rituals are performed. The largest show of participation observed was in 1990 when a large-scale passageway was constructed as a part of the opening ceremony. A majority of the people on the main floor of the civic center joined in the ceremony and walked through the ritual passageway from the old to the new year (see Figure 2.2). Similar to the stage performances at nineteenth-century ethnic festivals described by Bodnar (1987), these rituals are pointedly dramatic and didactic (see also Scott 1987: 29).

In contrast with the private celebrations 'look back' to elders and the past, the public celebration focuses its attention primarily on the role of youth in

Figure 2.2. Passageway scene at the New Year in St Paul, Minnesota. Photograph by Lynch.

leading the community in the United States. The stress of playing this role is a pointed focus of many of the stage presentations during the day. The conflicts inherent to the position of Hmong American teenagers as the generation caught in between Hmong and American culture were acted out in many ways at the festivals I attended. Plays about the theme were performed, and the speeches delivered by Hmong teenage leaders often centred on problems related to being both Hmong and American.

As in the private celebration, cloth is invested with symbolic meaning. In contrast to the home celebration where American styles of dress are typically worn, traditional styles of dress are emphasized at the public celebration. Dress styles influenced by or derived from Lao Hmong dress styles are generally worn only to the public celebration and are most consistently worn by Hmong youth. Just as teenagers and young adults are the most active at the public celebration so too they are most heavily adorned for the occasion. They choose their dress styles to fit the role they are playing either on stage or on the auditorium main floor. An interviewed Hmong teenager told me, 'At the New Year if we do something Hmong we were Hmong clothes, and if we do something American we were American clothes' (AL-F-03), indicating a conscious association of dress with cultural identity and/or situation. The teenagers generally wear Hmong-style dress for stage events that express pride in their Hmong heritage, such as singing a traditional song. They also tend to wear versions of Hmong traditional dress (females) or Hmong-inspired Euro-American dress (males) when they participate in the courtship ritual ball-toss game. American-style dress is worn for the evening dances and for stage events focused upon their lives in the United States. Dress worn in the evening tends to be purchased rather than hand-sewn and is often worn for other formal events throughout the year.

As in the case of the private celebration, textiles are used to express the integration of Hmong and American culture. In the private celebration, everyday American-style dress is moved into the Hmong world through ritual transformation by inclusion in the traditional cloth bundle symbolizing the past year. In the public context, Hmong-style dress and American-style dress are transformed to express the intermix of the two cultures.

There are dramatic contrasts between the dress ensembles worn by males and females to the New Year. Young men tend to wear Euro-American-style dress transformed to express Hmong pride and identity. In contrast, young women tend to wear more traditional styles which include American accents and trims. In both cases an intermix of the two cultures results. In the next two chapters I will describe and analyze dress styles worn by teenage Hmong Americans to the New Year.

3

Dressed to be Successful in America: Models of Masculinity at Hmong New Year

The Ball-toss as Ritual Courtship

The Hmong New Year is an annual celebration which, in Laos, traditionally fell at the end of the agricultural year. Families gathered to celebrate the harvest and prepare, through ritual actions, for the beginning of the year. Dates of the public New Year celebrations in communities throughout the United States are staggered to allow families to attend many of the festivals. In St Paul, Minnesota, the public New Year takes place over the Thanksgiving weekend in a large civic center and focuses primarily on teenagers and young adults. The New Year in Laos was the time of year when families gathered together to bring young people into contact with potential mates from other villages. As young people had to marry outside of their own clan, this was one of the few times they could meet potential marriage partners. In the American context, courtship is still a primary function of the event. The celebration in St Paul draws Hmong Americans from throughout the United States due to the large population of Hmong in the area which allows for a larger selection of marriageable females. Males from as far away as California come to the New Year in St Paul attempting to become acquainted with potential mates. A teenage girl said that potential mates from out-of-state ask for addresses so 'they can write to you or get to know you. That is a way to get to know you' (AL-F-01).

The courtship ritual ball-toss game played at the New Year in Laos is still played in the United States and is one way for young people to get acquainted. The game is played by male and female partners that stand across from each other and exchange turns throwing either a hand-made or tennis ball back

Figure 3.1. White Hmong men's dress. Photograph from Cubbs (1986).

and forth. Partners stand beside other players and form long lines, men on one side and women on the other. As the ball is tossed back and forth, I observed young people bantering back and forth and getting to know each other. In Laos the young men and women sang a style of call-and-response poetry which established levels of intimacy between the coupled players. Small numbers of couples still know how to chant the traditional poetry, but most converse back and forth on themes common to other young American people their age. Teenagers told me that communication between males and females is still the principle reason they play ball-toss. When asked about why he took part in the ritual one male teenager said: 'It is to communicate with girls. That is the only way we can meet new girls. You first of all have to test her mind. He has to find out if she can do what he wants. If she cannot do what he wants, they do not marry' (AL-M-03).

Therefore in both modern guise and historical time, the New Year festival is a ritual event focused upon presenting young men and women of marriageable age to each other and to the community. The New Year ball-toss ritual is an event to be dressed for in order to attract positive evaluations of character and appearance from the opposite sex and their families. Marriage partners are lifelong companions and, as such, must fulfill not only an attractive function, someone you have sexual desire for, but also must be able to succeed within the culturally determined gender roles of the community.

Hmong American New Year, as an ethnic festival, is a ritual focused upon reformation rather than re-enactment. It is a classic example of Turner's formative concept of ritual. As summarized in Chapter 1, in contrast with the notion of rituals presenting a crystallization of cultural values and traditions, Turner argues that ritual can have a generative as well as sustaining function. In other words, a ritual's symbols not only express the values and orientations of the past, but also change to express the concerns and values of the present. Hmong Americans, in the midst of cultural change, use dress worn in the New Year as a symbol to express and debate versions of cultural and gender identity.

To be Young, Male, and Hmong: Problems and Issues

The versions of male gender constructed through dress and behavior, and displayed at the New Year are influenced by problems and issues related to formulating Hmong American male gender roles in the United States. While American models of masculinity are often the base of male style displayed at the New Year, each is affected in some significant sense by historical models of Hmong masculinity. This fits with research done in public schools in St Paul in the 1980s (Sonsalla 1984) which concluded that Hmong students were adamant in their commitment to maintain cultural integrity despite their immersion in an American school system and by extension, American culture.

As outlined in the preceding background chapter, families in Laos were traditionally led by male elders. The central importance of the family in Hmong culture and the traditional role of male elders as leaders form the background for the conflicts which will arise as male gender roles are transformed to include young male leadership positions. The following section of this chapter will describe how conflict between generations is affecting male gender role construction, followed by a discussion of how dress worn to the New Year expresses newly emergent versions of Hmong American male gender identity.

Conflict Between Generations

The following excerpt is from the opening of Scene 8 in a play written as a part of the Hmong American Partnership Youth Program in St Paul Minnesota:

> For those of us who grow up in America, we find ourselves with one foot in ancient tradition, and one foot in modern America. School. Home. Being American. Being Hmong. As we grow up, the two cultures grow farther and farther apart. And the more you have to spread your legs, the more you lose your balance. We are blending into American life. Sometimes people want us to blend too fast, too much, too soon. Sometimes people don't want us to blend at all (Meyer et al. 1991)

The words point toward a major problem in the Hmong American community. To be Hmong is to be a member of a family. Again words from the play, 'To be Hmong is to be with family . . . Mother, father, sister, brother, aunt, uncle, grandmother, grandfather. Family is always more important than the individual' (Meyer et al 1991: 7). To be a member of a family as a newly relocated Hmong American is a struggle because older family members are not conversant in the American lifestyles of their children. Young Hmong Americans are growing up in a different world than their elders and while they value their cultural heritage, it is foreign to them because it is a part of a past they never experienced.

The chasm separating the two generations is exacerbated by the immigration and resettlement patterns of the Hmong Americans in St Paul and Minneapolis. Unlike other Southeast Asian groups, the Hmong exodus to the United States stretched over a fifteen year period. Families were slowly reunited in the United States. As new families arrived in the United States, their relatives often found housing for them in their own apartment complexes or neighborhoods, thus building up homogenous and bounded Hmong American enclaves within the larger metropolitan area. Within Minneapolis and St Paul, most Hmong American families live in concentrated pockets in lower-income inner-city neighborhoods or within federally subsidized apartment complexes in which the dominant ethnic population is Hmong. While a small number of Hmong American teenagers and children attend private and suburban schools, most are concentrated in inner-city schools with English as a Second Language Programs specifically directed toward Hmong children.

The prevalence of resettlement within homogenous immigrant neighborhoods, coupled with concentrations of Hmong youth in inner-city schools, have created vastly different life experiences for the young and old. Hmong American elders staying home all day are able to live in extended family groupings much as they did in Laos and thus are relatively undisturbed by outside American culture. In marked contrast, teenagers attend public schools and are in daily contact with larger American society.

My interviews with Hmong American teenagers and Daniel Detzner's (1990) interviews with elders revealed substantive differences in how new American life is experienced by the two generations. Elderly Hmong Americans often expressed feelings of loneliness and isolation. Many said they depended heavily upon younger members of their family to be liaisons between themselves and the American community. Teenagers vividly expressed the difficulties inherent in bridging the gap between Hmong and American culture. These teenagers, who characterized themselves in English as the 'in-between generation,' daily experience the contrast between the world within the Hmong community and the American world at school.

In its more positive guise this split between the old and young results in mutual respect and aid. More typically the demands of relocation and adaptation have divided Hmong families into three distinct generations, each having their own milieu and adjustment problems. Teenagers are swept into a demanding daily routine dominated by school while elders remain at home talking among themselves and caring for the younger children in the family. Meanwhile, the middle generation serves as a liaison between the outside world and the community and often financially supports the two other generations.

Generational differences in leadership roles have been consistently noted in Hmong refugee and immigration literature. Beginning with William Smalley's (1986) work in the refugee camps of Thailand, a duality of leadership was found wherein male elders retained ultimate authority within the community but the young were charged with leadership roles involving contact with outside agencies and individuals. Smalley argues that the roots of this duality can be traced to the breakdown of pre-existing clan-based social structures as a result of the war and relocation in the refugee camps. Hmong families were forced to break into small groups as they were fleeing from Laos in order to avoid detection. When they reached the camps, they were not settled according to clan but rather by arrival dates which thus created a fragmented settlement in which traditional family-based leadership was problematic.

One of the few intact social groupings within a particular Thai camp was a reunited group of 600 youth educated in the urban enter of Vientiane. As a result of their education and exposure to urban life, the students were natural liaisons between outside sources of aid and the Hmong community within the refugee camp. As one of the few cohesive Hmong social groups able to communicate with the Lao and American aid community, many of these students rose to positions of prominence, and later became middle-generation community leaders in the United States.

Generational differences in leadership roles which developed in the Hmong refugee camp community are also evident in research conducted in Hmong communities in the United States. Both John Finck (1982) and Douglas Olney (1988) stress generational differences in leadership roles in their research. Finck writes of the differences between the power held by male elders and the power held by younger men in a Hmong American community in Rhode Island:

> Clan leadership pivots on age. 'We are your children,' began Doua Yang, a young, bilingual man, himself the father of three, to the clan leaders. When the elders speak, the community responds. Last winter several hundred Hmong assembled for a community meeting on two days word-of-mouth notice, nearly filling the Veterans Auditorium. The older clan leaders – who have the political power to mobilize their community – rely on the younger bilingual men for the path through the American woods. The younger men have ideas but not the community respect which only the elders may confer. (1982: 25)

Olney's research also uncovered similar generational differences in leadership roles.

Alluded to, but not focused on, by the reviewed literature is the contrast between the sources of power behind the older and younger generation of Hmong leaders. Older leaders have access to information about Hmong culture that the younger generation feels is important to learn in order to maintain their Hmong identity. On the other hand, the younger generation has more completely absorbed an intuitive understanding of American culture, an understanding necessary to building a new life in the United States.

Text drawn from the interviews conducted with Hmong American elders and Hmong American teenagers reveals an awareness of the value of the knowledge held by youth and Hmong Americans respectively. Older Hmong Americans tend to feel trapped by their inability to survive on an everyday basis without the help of their younger relatives. Simple tasks like shopping or taking the bus are made difficult primarily because older Hmong Americans do not know how to speak or read English. Perhaps more significantly, older generation Hmong Americans expressed concern about being unable to help their children learn how to lead successful lives in the United States. When asked what important problems he had in the United States one elderly man answered:

> I don't have no one that help me to give better advice to teach or show my children. No one show my children to do this or do that, because I'm not educated and don't have a good idea to educate my children. (Detzner 1990)

Thus the traditional role of the male elder as a giver of wisdom, a conduit through which younger family members learn how to negotiate their way through life successfully, is seriously undermined by the compromised roles of male elders in American culture.

In interviews, elder Hmong Americans repeatedly spoke of the necessity of turning responsibility for future leadership over to the young people being educated in American schools. Teenagers, on the other hand, consistently expressed the feeling that they did not know enough about their own culture to participate fully in Hmong community life. Many teenagers expressed respect for peers who know how to sing the poetry traditionally chanted as part of the ball-toss but few Hmong American teenagers still practice the art form. Large Hmong American crowds surrounded singers at the New Year celebration in 1989 and 1990 indicating the once common art is now a rare novelty that draws the attention of interested outsiders and insiders.

Throughout the teenage interviews, elder males are consistently referred to as knowledgeable about Hmong culture and therefore worthy of respect and capable of playing key leadership roles within the Hmong community. The differing attitudes of the young toward middle and elder generation leaders were aptly captured in an interview with a teenage boy. When asked if the clan leader is always the oldest male in the family the boy replied:

> No, not necessarily the oldest, just the clan leader that can lead the family. For example he knows how to speak English, he knows how to write, he has high education. (AL-M-03)

When this question was followed by another asking if young leaders could also lead the rituals during the New Year the boy said:

> Oh, no. The only one who actually does the ceremony is old people. Old people that have certain words to say. Those young people mostly do not know how to say. (AL-M-03)

As Finck and Olney found in their research, while the role of the cultural go-between is assigned to younger-generation leaders much of the real power remains vested in the elders due to the knowledge they have accumulated over time. While both teenagers and elders interviewed were interested in the experiential knowledge carried by the other, both generations expressed feelings that the information was in a significant sense inaccessible to them given the harsh realities of their lives. Teenagers are busy balancing school, work, and family responsibilities and have little time to spend with their elders. As a result both generations suffer a loss: one of the world of the past and one of the world of the future.

Related to the erosion of traditional patriarchal leadership by elders is a problem of juvenile delinquency. As teenage males abandon the patterns of behavior of the past and attempt to adopt American standards of behavior they often get lost in terms of moral direction resulting in current youth delinquency and crime. Wendy Walker-Moffat (1995), in discussing the growing problem of juvenile delinquency in the Hmong American community, highlights the erosion of traditional clan-based patterns of leadership, as a core of the problem. Traditional leadership was hierarchical and patrilineal. As respect for elders and their knowledge declines, the security of a community led by commonly held cultural values erodes. One result of eroding respect for traditional models of masculinity is that the Hmong American teenage males struggling to define cultural notions of male gender role most often use American models as points of departure. These models stress individualism and are in conflict with traditional Hmong ideals focusing on family-based loyalty and communal definitions of success.

Dressing for Success, on Hmong American Terms

Core conflicts expressed in the versions of dress I observed at the New Year related to the preceding discussion include balancing expression of group and individual identity. Much more than young Hmong American women, young men use Hmong and American dress elements to express an individual sense of style. This emphasis upon developing a distinct sense of style is linked to the pressure they feel in America to succeed on their terms as individuals. The traditional Hmong model of group identity and success is challenged by these dress styles that often place the highest level of emphasis on individual expression over group affiliation.

As outlined in the previous background chapter, different Hmong dress styles for men were historically associated with different regions of Laos and Thailand and with different linguistic sub-groups. The clearest distinctions existed between the two broad categories of Green and White Hmong dress, which in turn corresponded to the two major linguistic sub-groups. White Hmong men wore black shirts with blue cuffs and black flared pants. In Figure 3.1 the man has substituted a more American-style white shirt and black vest for the more traditional white Hmong black shirt. Accessories included a dramatic pink or red waist sash, narrow coined belts and black skullcaps with red topknots. Green Hmong men's pants were also black but were cut large with a low crotch and fitted ankles. They also wore dark-cuffed shirts and black skullcaps (Figure 3.2). Dress, therefore, played the role of marking group identification with very little emphasis placed upon individual expression or development of a distinct sense of style.

Figure 3.2. Green Hmong men's dress. Photograph from Cubbs (1986).

Related to the above conflict between individual or group identity are mixed feelings toward hegemonic measures of male success in the United States. The Hmong American youth I talked to had ambivalent feelings about normative American definitions of male success. Many had become disillusioned with school and with the American education system as they observed peers graduating from high school unable to get good white collar positions or compete successfully for college assistance or scholarships. Suit styles were strongly correlated in the minds of these young men with attaining the American dream ideal of a good job and a home, but many had doubts concerning their ability to succeed on these terms.

Finally young men were trying to balance an interest in expressing modernity through fashion and style, with a strong sense of loyalty to their traditional past. New definitions of male leadership in the community focused largely on ability to embrace modern American life through access to technology, resources, and education. But at the same time traditional models of success based on knowledge of traditional religious and cultural practices, as embedded in the leadership of male elders, is still important to these young men. The result is a rich mix of traditional and modern dress influences in styles worn by young men to the New Year as they try to appear as modern and stylish as possible while at the same time expressing commitment to shared Hmong traditions and history.

Models of Masculinity Presented at the New Year

An aesthetic emphasis placed on fine dressing is fundamentally based in the very structure of New Year rituals of renewal. Finely sewn new clothing made expressly for the New Year is worn through the passageway marking new life and emerging possibility. New clothing is bright and full of contrast. Old clothing is dull and faded with little contrast. In order to be well received by the community and by your ancestors you must enter the New Year adorned in bright symbols of prosperity and growth; that is properly sewn and fully decorated New Year apparel. While young men attending the New Year enact differing versions of masculinity, they all express a pride in their appearance that is embed in traditional meanings of the New Year.

Four versions of masculinity emerged as distinct as I reviewed dress styles I observed at the New Year over the course of several years. The hegemonic model of masculinity as expressed through ensembles based upon the American business suit was the most common style of dress worn by young men participating in the ball-toss courtship ritual. Counter-hegemonic dress styles were growing in popularity. A consistent but small group of young men wore ensembles expressing commitment to traditional models of masculinity. Finally a sprinkling of young men wore lively ensembles heavily influenced by American popular culture.

The Hegemonic Model of Masculinity   The Hmong male version of the hegemonic ideal is influenced by the historical Hmong aesthetic favoring bright colors, shiny fabrics and a 'fancy' appearance for men as well as women. Being well dressed and accessorized in Laos was a mark of being from a good family that could provide new and special hand-sewn New Year apparel to its family members. Men wearing fine apparel were a reflection of their wives, and mothers, sewing skills. Finely sewn and decorated apparel was associated with cultural integrity and industriousness. As a reflection of Hmong aesthetics, conventional American suit styles are altered by Hmong wearers and sewers to achieve a more Hmong-style look. Suits are cut to mimic traditional pant and short jacket styles (see Figure 3.3). They are also

Figure 3.3. Hegemonic model of masculinity. Photograph by Lynch.

sewn from flashier fabrics than are most American suits. Decorative brooches and string ties, featuring shiny affects, customize the look and create a distinctive Hmong-style suit ensemble (see Figure 3.4). Therefore, while hegemonic models of masculinity appearing at the New Year are strongly influenced by American business apparel, they also have roots in traditional Hmong aesthetic patterns. While the young men can easily be recognized as wearing dress styles common in the United States they remain wed to their traditional past through fabric choices and decorative detail that link them to a tradition of fine sewing and shiny visual effects. In addition, the suit pays homage to the past in terms of cut and style. For example, coats tend to be cut closer and shorter than their mainstream American counterparts.

Counter-Hegemonic Models of Masculinity Counter-hegemonic models of masculinity are characterized by what Alfred Alder has defined as 'protest masculinity' (Connell 1995). This version of masculinity can emerge out of a childhood of powerlessness and results in an exaggerated show of male potency typically expressed as a collective response to marginalization. Michael Brake (1985), in his work on British youth culture, discusses the relationship between the marginal dress styles adopted and the youth's

Figure 3.4. Example of men's New Year accessories (string ties and brooches). Photograph by Lynch.

disregard for hegemony and its core value of paid labor as a symbol of successful masculinity:

> The cat revolts against the low paid work of the ghetto . . . he lives on his wits by hustling. Cool and aloof, ridiculing the 'square', he is an 'operator' completely cynical about the motivations of others . . . costume is used to convey an essential symbolic class and ethnic message. (128)

Carol Tulloch's (1993) study of British black street style points out that, while first-generation British blacks dressed in conventional dress for success models of hegemony, second-generation blacks, who had experienced discrimination, rebelled against normative definitions of masculinity and developed a 'striking, wild-style mien' (89) that spread into other countries including the United States.

Similarly, in my study of Hmong youth, the hegemonic ideal of masculinity dominated the early New Year celebrations I attended, but counter-hegemonic dress styles grew in popularity and appeal over the course of the four years I attended the New Year. Urban street culture and related dress styles began to affect the dress of male youth at the later New Year celebrations. The style was slick, again affected by interest in shiny fabrics, and dominated by the color black (see Figure 3.5). As in the hegemonic models of masculinity that developed in the Hmong community, American menswear styles were used as a point of departure, but Hmong attitudes toward decorative detail infuse the ensembles with a distinctly Hmong American look.

Figure 3.5. Counter-hegemonic model of masculinity. Photograph by Lynch.

Traditional Model of Masculinity A small but significant number of young men purposefully wear versions of Hmong-style dress to the New Year. These young men tend to be better educated; some are attending college, and profess to wearing Hmong dress styles in an effort to keep traditional Hmong culture alive. These young men are often conscious that key cultural and historical aspects of their identity are being lost or compromised through the adoption of American culture and ideals. These ensembles worn by young men, however, tend to be highly influenced by American styles. Business-style vests, which have no historical roots in traditional dress styles, are common. They tend to be made of shiny fabrics and heavily decorated with handwork or handsewn belts (see Figure 3.6)

I refer to these styles as 'new style' traditional ensembles in contrast with traditional ensembles that are modelled on historical prototypes. Young men wearing these ensembles generally make a point to dress in Hmong style for the New Year and tend to take great pride in their appearance. Having new and different versions of traditional dress for the New Year every year is important to this group. Despite the fact that these styles are clearly new interpretations of the past and affected by American dress styles, young men wearing these ensembles are adamant regarding the authenticity of their

Figure 3.6. Traditional model of masculinity. Photograph by Lynch.

ensembles. Mothers and other female relatives typically sew the apparel and are held in high regard by the young men. It is thus clear that while new and changing fashions appeal to these young men, they want the clothing sewn by women steeped in tradition and knowledgeable of past Hmong dress styles.

American Popular Culture Models of Masculinity   A fourth small group of young men respond to questions about their dress with less serious answers than those committed to presenting a more traditional appearance. They appear to take delight in wearing fancy dress to the New Year celebration, much in the same way American teenagers take delight in wearing formal attire to high school dances. Many of these dress styles appeared heavily influenced by American popular culture as seen in music videos and on television (see Figure 3.7). While elements of traditional Hmong dress are often integrated into these ensembles, the importance of the ensemble being linked to past traditions is not emphasized or even recognized by many of the teenagers I interviewed. These young men are interested in striking a modern pose at the New Year and their ensembles are appreciated as bold reinterpretations of New Year apparel to fit the new American context.

Figure 3.7. American popular culture models of masculinity. Photograph by Lynch.

Summary and Interpretation

Jennifer Hochschild's (1995) analysis of the underlying premises of the American dream surmises that American definitions of success are fundamentally based on radical individualism. Achievement, particularly for minority groups, is commonly marked by leaving the family and community of origin and taking off on one's to tackle and overcome obstacles. The story of the young man that strikes out on his own, leaves home and family, and achieves success, is a fundamental American myth that still motivates and directs many American men. This notion of success is in direct conflict with traditional Hmong values which emanate out of working toward family and community-based success and sacrificing individual desires and successes for the good of the whole.

All four of the dress styles worn by young men as they take part in the traditional ball-toss ritual at the New Year reflect an attempt to express commitment or reaction to the conflict between traditional male gender construction with its strong emphasis on family, respect for elders, and cultural knowledge; and the dominant American male gender construction focused on individual accomplishment and productive ability in the workplace. The most popular and widely worn style embraces the hegemonic ideal making only token references to Hmong tradition with additive trims, shiny fabrics, and suit styles. A second category of dress are counter-hegemonic styles that are reactions to both American and Hmong expectations. Ethnic identity remains a part of visual appearance in that shiny fabrics are emphasized. A third type of male dress is linked in the mind of the wearer to traditional dress styles. These ensembles, while self-consciously chosen and worn to underscore commitment to the past, are typically structurally rooted in American dress styles, as most consist of vest and pant combinations. The fourth style appears inspired by American popular culture and freely mixes traditional elements and trims with a range of American influences to create flamboyant and attention-grabbing visual statements of Hmong and American identity. All four models of masculinity remain rooted in traditional aesthetics which favor more decorative and shiny effects than found in typical American menswear.

Despite the contradiction between traditional Hmong and American notions of success, a majority of young Hmong American men choose to dress for the courtship ritual ball-toss in American menswear styles symbolizing commitment to the American hegemonic ideal, rather than wearing Hmong styles which would mark allegiance to group identity. Suit styles are the most common form of apparel worn by young men, and most young men and their female peers feel it is the most physically attractive and appropriate style for men to wear for the New Year. Suit styles tend to be cut to create silhouettes mirroring historical models of Hmong male dress, but the fundamental components of a traditional Euro-American business suit dominate the visual impression created by the ensemble.

The dialogue created by dress expressing all four versions of Hmong American masculinity raises questions about the flexibility of tradition, the importance of the past in constructing the present, and the new roles to be played by young men in American culture. The two most fundamental issues visually expressed and debated through dress are the emergence of young men as leaders within the community (accompanied by the erosion of the power of the elders in the community) and the conflict between the need to mark and honor group identity while at the same time striving to achieve individual recognition and success. The range of dressed appearance at the New Year expresses different solutions to these conflicts. As the young men appear and their dress is evaluated and discussed by the community, new versions of masculine gender formulate and emerge.

Dress styles worn by young men as they take part in the courtship ritual ball-toss express their position as young adults caught between two worlds: the Hmong world, stressing commitment to group and family success, and the American world stressing success defined by individual initiative even to the extent of abandoning group identity. As young men attempt to balance these two versions of success they use their dress at the New Year as a means of exploring different gender options and asserting their new Hmong American identity.

4

I am Hmong, I am American, I am a Hmong American Woman

Similar to their male counterparts, young women go to the New Year dressed to attract the attention and positive regard of their male peers, especially, and their families. Young women, as traditionally the more passive participants in courtship, are evaluated more intensely and therefore more care goes into presenting them as marriageable to the community and to potential suitors. While much of the debate surrounding male gender construction centers on new and old styles of leadership and new and old definitions of success, the debate for women focuses on appropriate roles for women at home and in the outside world.

New Year, as a focus of courtship within the community, becomes a logical arena in which to express the conflict surrounding appropriate gender roles for Hmong American women. The courtship ritual ball-toss has always been a ritual in which men have courted, evaluated and chosen their brides. Teenagers and young adults still meet potential spouses from their own and distant communities at the New Year. Male and female college students return home for the celebration. Many have brought home new ideas concerning female gender roles as a result of moving away from home and going to college, and they discuss and debate these ideas with schoolmates and peers from other communities. Dress becomes a visual expression of the debate.

Like their male peers, teenage females visually express ethnic pride through wearing traditional dress, but they also express attitudes toward Hmong and American gender roles through the range of choices they make in their New Year apparel. Like their male counterparts, dress worn to participate in the courtship ritual ball-toss becomes not only a statement of ethnic identity, but of gendered identity as well.

While young men and women both wear traditional styles to the New Year, many more females than males wear dress inspired by the past. As stated in the previous chapter, most young men wear dress suits modeled on

Figure 4.1. White Hmong female dress. Photograph from Cubbs (1986).

the Euro-American business suit. In contrast, most young women wear versions of traditional Lao Hmong dress. Similar to men's styles, when living in Laos women's dress styles were determined by sub-group membership. Again, the two main categories were Green and White Hmong. The dress of White Hmong women (see Figure 4.1) included a white pleated skirt with black leggings worn with a black shirt with blue cuffs and front edging. A rectangular collar at the back of the shirt was heavily decorated with embroidery and appliqué. The ensemble included a black apron and was worn with belts adorned with silver coins. In contrast, the dress of a Green Hmong woman (see Figure 4.2) customarily included a pleated skirt dominated

Figure 4.2. Green Hmong female dress. Photograph from Cubbs (1986).

visually by a wide central panel of blue batik work and decorated with appliqué and embroidery. Green Hmong women wore dark shirts similar to the White Hmong women, but their collars were worn with the decorative panel face down. Both groups of women wore a version of a dark wrapped turban, which generally featured a black and white striped turban tie.

White and Green Hmong distinctions are not emphasized in Hmong American New Year's dress. As I will discuss in the following chapter, teenagers feel free to draw from all sub-group styles when they put together their New Year ensembles. However, two distinctly American styles of traditional New Year's apparel emerged as dominant styles as I researched women's

Figure 4.3. Old-style female traditional dress. Photograph by Lynch.

dress at the celebration. The first style, which I refer to as 'old-style traditional dress' (see Figure 4.3) is characterized by relatively conservative use of American trims and accessories, the wearing of a dark turban headdress, a large densely pleated skirt, an apron, and heavy layering of the waist (see Figure 4.4). The second style of dress, which I refer to as 'new-style traditional dress' is characterized by liberal use of shiny American trims, the wearing of a heavily ornamented hat, a slightly less bulky skirt, and significantly lighter layering of the waist (see Figure 4.5).

Figure 4.4. Old-style female traditional dress. Photograph by Lynch.

In the following section of this chapter I will discuss conflicts underlying the reconstruction of female gender for the Hmong community in the American context. I will then explain how these conflicts are expressed, debated, and partially resolved in the two versions of traditional New Year apparel worn by young women as they take part in the courtship ritual ball-toss.

Figure 4.5. New-style women's traditional dress. Photograph by Lynch.

To be Hmong, American, and Female: Problems and Issues

Both the male and female youth I interviewed introduced the topic of conflict centered on women's roles in Hmong American families and among peer groups of young people. As a part of my fieldwork, I joined a group of male and female Hmong teenagers on a camping trip. The problematic relationship between teenage Hmong American males and females was a playful but pointed focus of joking on the camping trip. The problems expressed centered on trying to reconcile traditional Hmong gender roles with customary American gender constructions. One female leader on the trip was a strong-willed high school senior who made a special point of prodding the boys to help with the camp chores, chores which old-style Hmong women would have customarily done in the households in which the boys were raised. A feisty pair of female tent mates played an on-going joking game throughout the two days in which one played the role of the old-style wife and one played the role of the old-style husband. To the amusement of their audience, the husband repeatedly bossed the wife about in an exaggerated display of dominance.

During an extended interview with me, a teenage boy expressed his awareness of, and sensitivity to, the dramatic differences between women's roles in Lao Hmong society and women's roles in the United States:

I have feelings about that [women's roles]. I guess I have been brought up here and I see American women's role, the Hmong just had it differently. Women are always second, they eat second, they do everything second. The men are sort of in charge. I have a slightly different thought about that because I have been raised here. (AL-M-05)

While boys can intellectually accept that their teenage female peers have different roles to play in the United States, many male, as well as female, youth have problems reconciling older and emerging gender roles for women. In addition to conflicts concerning appropriate work roles in the family, conflicts between, and within, the males and females centered on issues of marriage, sexuality, and definitions of female success.

Marriage

The questions surrounding appropriate male and female gender roles in the United States have caused internal problems within the community. Central issues were the freedom to date and appropriate age of marriage. Hmong girls, like other American teenagers, want to be able to go on dates and attend extra-curricular school social functions. The custom of arranged marriages and chaperoned dating, with which their parents grew up, no longer fits the American context. In regard to marriage, the conflict between Hmong custom and the American legal system poses problems. With parental approval, early marriage (before the age of fifteen) continues to be practiced in Minnesota, despite Minnesota laws prohibiting girls under sixteen from marrying. Despite these legal obstacles, Hmong American teenagers said that common marriage ages for girls were between fifteen and eighteen. Teenage females expressed concern over the pressure they felt from their families to follow the dictates of the past by marrying and beginning their families while still teenagers.

Teenage females bound for college often expressed conflict over delaying their marriage to get an education. Their concerns are double-edged. First, the opportunity to meet and marry a husband is greater when the girls are still in high school. If they wait, they risk being labeled too old and no longer desirable. Second, teenage females realize that Hmong American men are often hesitant to marry women with higher levels of education than their own. As most Hmong American women want to marry within their own community, they often say that they hinder their chances to make an appropriate match by increasing their level of education. The following is a response given by a female teenager when asked whether she felt pressured to marry after graduating from high school, 'For the Hmong, sixteen is an old age to get married. I do kind of feel pressure that if I go to college I will never get married because I went to college' (AL-F-03). Bride prices, which are paid to the bride's family by the groom's family, are often said to decrease if the bride is well educated. This fundamental conflict, between wanting to marry and fulfill common Hmong expectations, and the desire to stay in school and conform to American standards for high-school-age women, places a burden of choice on young women which many find difficult to bear.

Sexuality

The adoption of American standards of sexual morality by some members of the Hmong American community has also caused some problems between young men and women. In 1991, for instance, two professional Hmong American men in Minnesota were convicted of criminal sexual misconduct; both men claimed to have had sexual relations with consenting Hmong American women (Hammond 1991). Another sexual assault case brought by a fourteen-year-old female against a nineteen-year-old male revealed that the young man acted, at least in part, as a result of exposure and misunder-standing of American attitudes and behaviors. According to Goldstein (1986) the young man felt 'his sexual aggression was a permissible blend of American and Hmong actions' (140) and he was thus confused by the legal results of his actions.

Similar to their male counterparts, appropriate sexual behavior for Hmong American teenage females is also in a state of flux and debate. At the 1991 Second Annual Conference of Hmong Women Pursuing Education held in Wisconsin, an older woman stood up and passionately said, "In Laos we lived in houses without windows and without doors to lock and our daughters did not get pregnant. Here there are windows and doors that lock and our daughters get pregnant." Middle-generation speakers at the conference made a point of telling mothers in the audience that they need to talk to their daughters about birth control, a controversial topic within the Hmong

American community. The high traditional value placed on fecundity, coupled with the traditional low marriage age, makes these girls particularly vulnerable to early pregnancy and bearing the burden of raising children while also trying to complete their education.

Definitions of Success

Hmong American women also have to balance Hmong and American notions of success. Lao Hmong female gender role was strongly embedded in the agricultural economic base of the culture. Fecundity (the ability to conceive and bear children) was integral to the women's role, because having many children was important as families needed to be large to provide the labor needed to farm. Physical strength and a heavy body type were associated with the ability to have children as well as to labor hard to help the family achieve success. To marry young and to have children, and thus be assured of a valued role within the community, remains important to Hmong American women. However, marriage and raising a family while still a teenager conflict with achieving success as measured on American terms. For instance, the young mothers whom I tutored at an area high school had to balance school work with motherhood and missed many days of school. The problem continues for those women who attend college. At the women's conference in Wisconsin, women enrolled in college repeatedly addressed the problem of finding affordable daycare for children.

Successful Hmong American women, aware of the gender-role stresses of their younger counterparts, attempt to provide support and guidance to the young women. Houa Moua, a prominent woman in the Wisconsin Hmong American community, gave the keynote address at the luncheon during the women's conference in 1991. She closed by telling a story expressing the message that young Hmong American women, though tempted to seek marriage partners outside the community, should remain true to self and true to the community and marry within their own ethnic group. The story, as translated, follows:

A rat wanted to marry the best and most powerful man in the world. The first man the rat chose to marry was the moon. But then she said to herself, the moon is not so powerful. The light of the moon can be covered by a cloud. I should marry the cloud. So the second man the rat chose to marry was a cloud. But then the rat said to herself, a cloud is not so powerful, a cloud can be pushed by the wind. So the third man the rat chose to marry was the wind. But then the rat said to herself, the wind is not so powerful, it cannot push the mountain. But then the rat said to herself, a mountain is not so powerful. A rat can gnaw a hole in a mountain. And so the rat decided to marry a rat.

The story was warmly received and drew out smiles of understanding from the all-female audience.

This story illustrates the fact that young Hmong American women are struggling hard not only to figure out who they are, but who they are in relationship to their male peers, their potential mates. They understand that they must respect the power of their own men in order to respect themselves and to contribute to the well-being and strength of the Hmong American community. But the role they are asked to play by their male peers is a difficult one. Hmong American teenage boys are American enough to want to marry an American-style woman, yet they also want a Hmong spouse, someone who will tether them to their own cultural roots. This frustration was voiced in the afternoon session of the Wisconsin conference when a young woman enrolled in college stood up and passionately declared: 'Hmong women go to college and [learn to] expect different things [in their lives]. Hmong men go to college and expect the same things from their wives.' Her comment indicated that educated Hmong American men prefer women similar to their mothers, women tied to the gender roles of the past. As a result, those Hmong American women who attend college are expected to fall back into the gender roles they were raised with, whereas young Hmong American men are encouraged to use their education to grow, change, and succeed on American terms. This difficult balance, between being American enough to succeed in the United States, yet Hmong enough to fulfill the role of being a bearer and keeper of culture, is expressed in the range of dress worn by Hmong American female youth to the New Year.

Hmong American New Year's Dress for Women

Traditional styles of Lao Hmong dress are worn by both young men and young women to the New Year, but more women than men choose to wear dress modeled after traditional Lao prototypes. Most of the girls prefer to wear American-style dress, yet feel an obligation to wear Hmong-style dress to recognize their cultural background. This response is typical, 'I prefer American clothes. But still I wouldn't mind wearing my Hmong clothes, because it is what I am, it is a part of me' (AL-F-06). As stated earlier, many young women wear a mix of sub-group styles to the New Year. Small numbers make a special point of dress entirely within a single sub-group tradition but most draw freely from the range of styles available from family members and sewers in the area.

A pleated wrapped skirt is the foundation for the ensemble. Green Hmong skirts, because of their bright color range achieved through batik (blue), embroidery and applique (reds and greens), are the most popular skirt in St Paul. Skirts are stored with approximately quarter-inch pleats sewn in place that are released prior to wearing to ensure a sharp, clean appearance. Short cuts to the traditional techniques of embroidery, appliqué and batik are common. Commercially printed fabric is now available that mimics the old-style patterns. White skirts, that are historically linked to White Hmong dress styles, are also worn. Most young women wear an undershirt of some kind covered by a jacket shirt style that overlaps for closure in the front. The shirt is a T-shaped garment with boxy sleeves and wide (approximately 2-inch) cuffs, typically in a contrasting blue or heavily decorated with handwork and added trim and sequins (see Figure 4.5). Long vertical apron styles are worn over the skirts. These aprons are decorated in the new-style ensembles and generally black in the traditional-style ensembles. Skirts, jackets and the apron are all held in place by heavily wrapping the waist with cloth, followed by a series of decorated sashes and purses. Coins are sewn to the sashes and purses creating an audio as well as visual effect of dynamism.

Headdress Styles and Meaning

Most Hmong American women continue to wear some version of headdress when they wear Hmong-style dress. Even older women seated on the balcony at the New Year wearing versions of American dress often complete their ensemble with a turban-style headdress, thus indicating a continued association of the turban with cultural identity. In terms of discussion and debate, headdresses emerged as controversial and important in terms of female gender construction. Therefore, within this section, I will devote specific attention to their meaning, usage patterns, history and style.

In Laos different versions of wrapped headdress were associated with distinct sub-groups of Hmong. As fieldwork progressed, I found that the two most common versions of women's headdress worn to the New Year by teenagers (and some older women) carried different meaning within the community. Both headdress styles are related historically to smaller sub-groups of Lao Hmong. The turban-style (Figure 4.3) is historically linked to the dress styles of a White Hmong sub-group. It is customarily a 12-foot length of dark maroon Vietnamese silk (Cubbs 1986) wound around the head to create a rounded dark form. The second style (Figure 4.6) is a rooster-style hat made of cotton and synthetic fabrics which rests upon, rather than wrapping around, the head. It is called rooster-style because of the shapes on the top resembling a cockscomb. The closest prototype to this style of hat exists in the Green Hmong tradition as a children's hat. Hats are usually purchased from sewers who have completed the basic construction of the

Figure 4.6. Detail rooster-style New Year hat. Photograph by Lynch.

hat and added the appliquéd and embroidered designs. Women within individual families then further decorate the hats with a range of trims including aluminum coins, metal balls, yarn pom poms, rickrack and sequins to create a visually complex and reflective surface.

The turban style is generally classified by Hmong Americans as 'old-style' Hmong, whereas the rooster-style hat is widely interpreted as 'modern' or 'new-style' Hmong. Typical comments on the two hat styles included this one from a teenage male when asked about the rooster-style hat, 'It is not really Hmong, it is just a couple years old, it is modernized Hmong' (AL-M-05). One girl (among many) when asked to compare the hat to her turban commented that her turban was 'more traditional' (AL-F-04). The classification of the turban as the more 'traditional' of the two headdress styles is not based upon costume history, as both turbans and hats have historical prototypes and could therefore be defended as traditional. Neither the hat nor the turban form was universally worn by all the Hmong sub-groups prior to their arrival in the United States; so neither has universal significance within the community in terms of patterns of historical use. Both are now worn as marks of more general Hmong American identity by women from all the formerly distinct Lao Hmong sub-groups, each having evolved from marking sub-group identity into symbols of more broadly-based Hmong identity.

Turbans are associated in the minds of the Hmong living in Minnesota with traditional systems of meaning. One older man directly tied the turban-style headdress to the world of the ancestors, dismissing the rooster-style hat as bound only to contemporary reality, 'The turbans are the custom. The hats are new things and are not from the ancestors' (AL-M-01). Even within a Green Hmong family who expressed pride in the rooster hat due to its relationship to their sub-group, the turban was deemed the more traditional of the two headdress styles. While the father told me that he liked the hats because he remembered similar hats being worn by children in his sub-group, he nevertheless assigned a more traditional label to the turban-style headdress arguing that the rooster-style hat was a more 'modern' choice for women living in the United States (AL-F-03).

Most young women reported that they wear both headdress styles for different occasions within the two-day New Year celebration. Female teenagers elect to wear the turban form when they are trying to please their relatives or other elders within the community or when they are making a public presentation of themselves as committed to Hmong history and culture. Teenagers often have arguments with their female relatives focused upon their desire to wear the hat rather than the turban to the New Year. The following quote in which a teenage female describes an exchange with her older aunt, captures this tension, 'Well, if I don't want to wear the turban and I am very determined not to wear it, she will give up and say "fine, you wear the hat"' (AL-F-03). Many of the Hmong Teen of the Year contestants I interviewed stressed that, as contestants, they were expected to pay respect to their cultural past by wearing older styles of Hmong dress. One female contestant wore a turban to the New Year for the first time when she competed for Teen of the Year. She expressed pride in the turban form, and said that it was 'unique ... it was more traditional' (AL-F-04). She had attended the New Year regularly before that, always wearing a hat. She commented that her parents preferred the turbans because the hats were 'too Americanized' (AL-F-04), but that she had always worn a hat in the past. The year she was interviewed by me she wore the turban for a part of the day, as she felt as a contestant for Teen of the Year she should dress as traditionally as possible. Another one of the contestants for Teen of the Year commented that while she wore her hat most of the day, when it came time to give her speech on stage she 'wore the turban with stripes [striped turban tie] because we were supposed to wear our most traditional stuff' (AL-F-01). Speeches given by the contestants tend to focus on the need to maintain cultural ties to the past as well as adjust to life in America, so wearing traditional styles of dress befits the message.

Most teenage girls, even if they admitted to liking to wear the turban to express commitment to the past, also wear the rooster-style hat to different events within the two-day celebration. In contrast to the traditional meanings of the turban-style, rooster-style hats are associated with fashion and with the casual American lifestyle many of the girls are trying to capture. They are the most popular form of headdress among the young women and teenage girls.[1] The hat's scalloped edge and active reflective surface are interpreted as fashionable, colorful and pretty by young Hmong American women. One young woman said she liked the hat better because, 'For me it is more fashionable. It has more color and is pretty. That is why I wear it. It is easy to put it on and take it off and put it on again. But the other one [the turban], if you mess it up you have to take it off and do it over again' (AL-F-03). Hmong American girls like the hats because they can pop them on their heads, thereby asserting independence from their older female relatives and, by association, independence from the dictates of the past. A girl wearing a new-style hat is on her own for the day, whereas a girl wearing a turban is usually the focus of continued scrutiny and attention as older female relatives evaluate, comment on and rewrap the turban throughout the New Year celebration. This freedom from adult intervention mirrors the independent lifestyle young Hmong American women think is appropriate in America. Like their peers at school, young Hmong American women want to socialize and date freely. Many want to make their own choices regarding marriage

---

1. Small numbers of Hmong American girls, particularly those who have given up many other aspects of Hmong culture, are committed to the turban because they associate it with authentic Hmong culture and the past. One female contestant, with a history of minimal involvement in Hmong cultural life in St Paul, said she liked the turban better because, 'It is more traditional and looks better. I don't like the hats. They are too new. I mean they are so contemporary, you know. I like the old' (AL-F-02). She was one of the few teenage females who dismissed the value of the hat.

and college plans. Wearing the hats makes them feel more independent, more modern, more fashionable.

In the arena of the New Year, the new-style hats are practical. The girls come to the St Paul Civic Center with suitcases filled with clothing changes for the various events during the day. The range of dress styles needed for the event is indicative of the multiple roles these young women play within their community. Teenage females are quick to match their style choices with specific events, using dress to express multiple identities and attitudes. Typical suitcases include different versions of Hmong-style dress as well as formal and casual American styles. As the girls change from Hmong style dress in the afternoon to American party clothes for the evening, the hats are easily put aside leaving the girl's hairdo relatively undamaged from an afternoon of wear. In contrast, when tightly wrapped turbans are unwound, the hair is flattened and difficult to style. This was often a source of complaint from the teenagers whom I watched change from Hmong to American-style dress in the public restrooms, preparing for the American-style dance in the evening.

Old-Style Traditional Dress

When combined with other old-style dress, the turban form helps to emphasize a rounded and relative plump ideal of beauty which was historically valued within the community. As stated previously, because a Lao Hmong woman's marriageability was strongly associated with her ability to work hard on the farm and her ability to have children, a sturdy healthy woman was highly regarded and prized. As can be seen in Figures 4.3 and 4.4, the waist area of old-style versions of Hmong traditional dress is heavily layered creating a bulky, strong image. The calves of the legs are also frequently wrapped to create the look of a heavy, solid leg. As succinctly and directly stated by a teenage girl during an interview, 'It [Hmong style dress] makes you look fat. When you are fat and you wear Hmong [dress] you look fatter' (AL-F-05). This idealization of the rounded body form fits well within the traditional definition of female success, as primarily focused upon child-bearing ability, good health, and hard physical labor.

The cultural meaning carried by old-style dress and the turban in particular is further supported by comparing the act of putting on and removing the turban with the ease of wearing the hat. Older women watching the New Year festivities from the Civic Center balcony, unwrap and rewrap their turbans without moving their eyes or attention from the stage show below. However, such practiced ability is rare among younger Hmong American women. The turbans are only worn for photographs and celebrations and few girls learn to wrap their own. As a result, young women are mostly

Figure 4.7. Young girl having her turban tied. Photograph by Lynch.

dependent upon their mothers and other older women to help them wrap their turbans properly. When a girl is having her turban tied, she typically rests her knees in a dependent pose in front of the person wrapping it for her (see Figure 4.7). The implied dependence is further amplified by the continual 'fixing of the young woman's turban' by mothers and other female relatives throughout the day. This dependency is a constant reminder to the teenage girls of the restrictions placed upon their lives by the dictates of female gender roles transmitted to them by their older female relatives. The act of being dressed by members of their family places these young women under the care [and control] of their elders, a position harkening back to the marriage and courtship patterns of Laos.

New-Style Traditional Dress

In contrast with the stylistic uniformity of the old-style traditional dress, new-style ensembles often express mixed visual messages. Young women,

Figure 4.8. Hmong girls dressed for the New Year. Photograph by Lynch.

trying to satisfy others as well as dress in styles that express their own versions of Hmong American identity often mix older-style elements into their ensembles. The results are ranges of dress styles from extreme versions that do not include headdress (see Figure 4.8) to fairly conventional layering of the waist combined with the rooster-style hat and perhaps high heels. Typical are visual effects that add apparent height to the body such as the wearing of high heels and the pointed rooster-style hat. Ensembles which combine the new style hat, less layering of the waist, and high heels conform much more closely to the slim Western ideal which many Hmong American girls are now attempting to attain. The pointed rooster-style hat, long hair, and high heels make the body appear longer and thinner. The decreased layering of the waist results in a leaner, more American look. The importance placed upon child-bearing and physical strength, key elements of the traditional definition of female role and success, are minimized in favor of an ideal stressing conformity to American notions of beauty and success.

Fashion impulses are also integrated into the ensembles in the form of new fabrics, trims, or accessories. Typically every year I was able to pick out important fashion-based elements indicating attention to a 'modern look' that characterized new-style ensembles. Red shoes and gloves were important accessories in 1990. Polka dot skirts became important the following year.

Figure 4.9. New style turban tie being worn as a leg wrap. Photograph by Lynch.

Hmong sewers and others within the community could trace the beginnings of the use of distinct fabrics and trims to specific sewers who had reputations as trendsetters. The decorative rather than striped turban ties that started out as a fashion impulse became an element in many aspects of Hmong American New Year's dress, eventually making their way into more traditional women's styles and men's popular culture ensembles (see Figure 4.9). At the close of my research in 1992 Chinese Miao dress styles were also beginning to influence women's New Year apparel as a result of travel of Hmong Americans to China in search of their past.

In general, new-style ensembles conform more closely to American ideals of beauty in terms of preferred body type, are more open to fashion impulses, and express higher degrees of individuality than the older-style ensembles. These characteristics of the new style when combined together challenge basic cultural principles underlying Lao Hmong society. Firstly, the dress style is fashion conscious, looking forward to the future rather than focusing attention on traditional values and rituals. Secondly, it is a style open to individual expression, therefore in conflict with basic Hmong ideals of family-based success and identity. Finally, the thinner ideal of beauty begins to challenge basic ways of measuring the value of a woman. The ability to have children and perform hard physical labor, both attributes of key importance within the Lao Hmong female gender role, are challenged by new styles and new versions of gender identity within the New Year.

Old-Style vs. New-Style Dress: Male Responses

Early in my research, interviews and observations among Hmong males revealed an association between the style of dress worn by young women and how they were evaluated by young men in regard to marriageability. For example, a teenage male said he liked girls better in Hmong clothes rather than American-style dress because 'it brings out the Hmong in the girls I suppose' (AL-M-01). Another male teenager said that he would not let his sister go to the New Year 'in American clothes because it is a way to celebrate our culture and if I see American clothes it is sort of saying that they are not valuing it as much anymore' (AL-M-05). In contrast, males tend to be judged less harshly for wearing American styles of dress to the New Year. Teenage girls often told me they thought the boys looked good in both American and Hmong dress. This response is typical, 'Some of the boys when they wear Hmong clothes, they look really good in them. Really dashing and everything, you know. They look OK in American clothes too, but it doesn't really matter. It is the same to me' (AL-F-03). This contrast makes clear that linkages to tradition (as expressed through dress) are seen within the Hmong American community as important components of female gender construction.

Males, particularly those who have lived in the United States for a significant period of time, generally prefer the turban headdress style for women. Teenage males are much more apt than their female counterparts to dismiss the rooster-style hats as 'simply American.' The value placed upon the hat is often negatively influenced by the fact that the boy judging it feels it is too 'Americanized.' For example, one boy said about the hats, 'I think it looks cheap' (AL-M-01), thus assigning the hand-made hat far less value than other items of dress worn by the young women. Men and boys who have recently moved to the United States were less judgmental. One young man told me that, 'I like them both [the hats and the turbans]. They are both pretty. But this [the turban] is the custom. But the [rooster] hat, they just made them up' (AL-M-02). His father also liked both styles but felt the turban matched 'the rest of the costume better' (AL-M-02).

The negative response to the hats and the leaner, more American look seems to be a learned response. In interviews, males who have lived in the United States for a number of years often associated women who wear Hmong-style dress to the New Year rituals with authenticity and cultural integrity. For example, when a young man was asked whether he preferred Hmong or American dress on Hmong American young women, he said:

I would probably say Hmong clothes. It is like, sometimes when the girls wear American clothing, it is not them you are looking at it is more their clothing. It is like they hide themselves behind their clothing. There are situations where a girl can have a lot of nice clothing but be so different. With Hmong clothes, it is like everyone wears the same and I don't know, it brings out the Hmong in the girls, I suppose. (AL-M-01)

The more Americanized hairstyles are also a source of controversy. Hairstyles are most noticeable when women wear the new-style hats. Hmong women's hair is typically dark and contrasts more vividly with the multicolored reflective hats than with the dark turbans. In addition, the style of the hat allows the wearer more experimentation and variety in hair dress than does the turban. Generally, women wearing the turban pull their hair into a topknot and cover it completely with the turban. Many of the males' negative comments about the hats centered on the fact that the women's hair was loose. For example, the following are comments from a male teenager:

My dad says the girls come here and wear the hats and their hair all hangs down and it covers their face and it doesn't show a lot of beauty. That is what the older generation is looking for and why they have the turbans to show off the beauty. All the girls [wearing the turbans] have their hair back. Now the girls come here and it is all hanging over their eyes. I think it looks cheap. (AL-M-01)

This points toward the role of women's dress and its evaluation by others in the expression of conflict centered upon female gender role in community. It is not simply that the boy and his father prefer the turban to the hat, but they feel the hat looks 'cheap.' Turbans, in contrast, are associated with beauty and value. Hats are associated with 'coming here' and with women losing beauty, losing value.

Even males who were willing to define their own extravagantly Americanized Hmong style dress as traditional were unwilling to define the hat as traditional. During an interview with a young man, I commented that the ensemble he had worn to the past New Year was quite a modern interpretation of the older styles. He replied, 'Yes, it is a modern interpretation' (AL-M-05). When I queried why he considered his own new-style dress traditional and yet dismissed the hats as 'not really Hmong,' he defended the authenticity of his own ensemble by saying that it was composed of the same basic dress components as in the past but 'just has different decorations' (AL-M-05). His comment indicates that the form, rather than the surface detail, made the connection with the past. In his mind the hats, being clearly a different form than the turbans, made a clear, formal break from old-style female dress. Despite her older brother's reservations concerning the authenticity of the hat, this young man's sister consistently wore the hat to the New Year, indicating different opinions within families as to appropriate Hmong headdress for women.

The young man's argument that the rooster-style hats are not traditional is an indication of the importance of formal characteristics in the debate centered on women's headdress within the Hmong American community. As both turbans and hats have historical prototypes, each could be defended as traditional. Nevertheless, as viewed by the community, the turban form worn by young Hmong American women marks cultural transmission and continuity, whereas the hat marks cultural change and transformation. The hat, decorated with sequins, lurex and other shiny objects reflects light and is associated with openness to change and a modern outlook. This is in sharp contrast with the dark-colored, round silhouette of the turban which symbolizes stability, links to a cultural past and more conservative interpretations of women's roles. Preference by many Hmong American women for the hat challenges the authority of males and elders who typically prefer and feel most confortable with the turban and its association with more conservative gender roles for women. The debate surrounding head coverings for women reveals differences of opinion regarding the appropriate roles for women to play in the Hmong American community.

Conclusion

Teenage Hmong American males' and elders' desires for young women to windround the cloth of tradition and appear bedecked in the old-style dress and turban points toward the role of women as ties to the past, ties to cultural history. Young women's insistence on making their own dress choices and donning hats expressive of change and transformation indicates the important role of dress in expressing the debate surrounding appropriate gender roles for Hmong women in American society. My research demonstrates that within ritual performances, objects not only reflect but help to formulate cultural systems (Geertz 1973). Debates surrounding women's New Year's dress choices help to create new roles for Hmong American women in the United States. As a Hmong American male college student or as an older relative struggles to accept (and find aesthetically pleasing) the wearing of a new-style hat by a teenage female, they are also struggling to accept the new roles she may play in the United States.

Visual art forms, especially those interrelated with the human body, are material embodiments of cultural worlds. As a result of the creation, perception, and evaluation of visual art forms, aspects of culture are transformed. As members of the Hmong American community develop new criteria for the judgment of female beauty, they also develop new criteria for what makes a good woman, a Hmong American woman, a woman who carries the treasures of the past on her back and embraces the new American world. The heated debates surrounding the value and authenticity of the rooster-style hat point toward the formative role of dress styles worn during the New Year ritual in the creation of Hmong American cultural identity. What is superficially discussed is the value of a hat; what is more significantly debated is the flexibility of Hmong cultural life in the American context. As Hmong Americans create, debate, and judge their own traditional dress, they simultaneously reformulate their culture in response to their new environment. They learn what it means to be a Hmong American by making and judging dress styles that reflect the past and mold the present.

In situations of cultural contact, in which men and women are struggling to mark ethnic integrity and express a flexible and realistic response to new circumstances, dress becomes a means of negotiating identity by using forms of dress that carry meaning from the past and negotiate meaning in the present. Newly emergent versions of gendered identity are formulated as the dressed body is presented and evaluated. In the following chapter, which will conclude the portion of this book devoted exclusively to Hmong American dress and gender, I analyze the concepts of tradition and ethnicity as they apply to Hmong American New Year's dress.

5

Invention of Tradition: Emergence of Ethnic Dress in America

A key concern of both young men and young women I worked with was maintenance of Hmong identity. Young adults returned to the New Year celebration in the St Paul Civic Center year after year because of a strongly felt need to make a public statement of Hmong identity. While on a daily basis many try hard to be as much like their American peers as possible, it was clear that being Hmong, including dressing Hmong, was important to these young people. The Hmong style dress worn by young men and women at the New Year symbolizes ethnic identity as well as ties to tradition and history. What is considered 'traditional' dress within the community varies with age and gender as does how dress is used to mark ethnic identity.

Invention of Traditional Dress in America

The following is taken from my fieldnotes. It aptly captures the value that Hmong Americans place on new versions of the old-style Hmong dress as well as the value many place on the dress of the past:

I am interviewing a teenage girl in her apartment in a subsidized housing complex. As we are talking her mother quietly comes down the stairs with a bundle of clothing and begins laying out old-style collars she brought with her when she was relocated to the United States from Thailand. The teenage girl is impatient first with her mother for interrupting the interview by laying out the collars, then with me for expressing interest in the old-style dress. 'These days we have nicer ones. If you would like to see them. We have nicer ones. These are really old and these the kids now, this generation would not wear those.' 'They don't like these?' I query. 'No,' the girl answers. 'They like the new ones because they are really pretty – the ones now are really pretty.' 'What do you like better about the ones now?' I ask. The answer is brief and to the point – one word 'colorful.' 'What is it,' I ask, 'you

71

don't like about the collars your mother brought from Laos?' She answers, 'Oh, I like them. It is just that I won't wear them. They show it is really an old style.' (AL-F-05)

'Fashion,' the new style, what does the *new* old-style Hmong dress mean to Hmong Americans? What does the word 'traditional' imply when we use it to describe the dress of others? What does it mean when we use it to describe our own dress?

The aesthetic preference for new versions of the old styles is fundamentally based in the very structure of New Year rituals of renewal. Old clothing sewn expressly for the New Year is worn through the passageway marking new life and emerging possibility. What is new is shiny, is bright, is full of contrast and color.[1] What is old is dull and faded with little contrast and subdued color. When you are new in the Hmong world you are wearing a shiny satin shirt (the placenta). When you die in the Hmong world you must return to your place of birth and wear your coat of satin (the placenta) into the world of the ancestors (Peterson, 1990: 189); this assures you a continued life, continual renewal and reincarnation.

Sally Peterson (1990) associates the contemporary Hmong American value placed on newness with the historic value placed upon keeping handwork clean in the adverse conditions in Lao hill country. She goes on to discuss the contemporary importance of the concept of newness as an evaluation criterion in judging the quality of handwork. She argues that the concept embodies notions of 'spiritual renewal, material abundance, and economic prosperity' (267). This is in keeping with the idea discussed above that the ability to provide new clothes for the family is a mark of economic prosperity and well-being. Women that are able to sew for their families help assure the spiritual well-being of the family for the coming year and visibly display the ability of the family to meet the material needs of its members. Peterson points out that the frequent use of plastic wrap to cover easily soiled handwork is an attempt to keep the dress decorations clean and new looking and therefore aesthetically pleasing.

Many of the teenagers I interviewed expressed preference for the new, the fashionable version of Hmong-style dress. For example, at the 1990 New Year, two young women I had known and observed at the New Year in both 1988 and 1989 showed me their hats. The hats were trimmed with a green trim I had not seen before. The two young women confidently pronounced that their hats were the 'new style' this year. While the form of the hat was

---

1. In the past, hand-woven hemp was polished to a shine in order to express the value that Hmong place upon the appearance of newness (Cubbs 1986).

similar to the hats of the past, the trim was distinct; and within the Hmong American community, the hats did stand out as a new and different version of the older style. Skirt styles also came in and out of fashion. In recent years White Hmong skirts suffered some loss of popularity in the community due to their relatively plain surface. Teenage girls tended to prefer the more brightly colored Green Hmong skirts. In 1990 I observed small numbers of White Hmong-style skirts sewn from polka dot print being worn. In 1990 textile artists in the community had set up tables selling the new-style polka dot print White Hmong skirts and many more young women were wearing them.

In the United States, it is the well-known artists who often start the new fashions. For example, I saw a well-known Hmong American textile artist wearing her own outfit to the New Year in 1990 featuring a distinct appliqué pattern. Later on in the day I saw a young man wearing initial teenage versions of that fashion, indicating that the style will probably show up on a greater number of teenagers the following year. The ready willingness on the part of older artists to experiment with new fabrics and trims indicates that the desire for the new is not purely an American phenomenon. After all, these women learned to sew and judge the quality of handwork in villages in Laos.

Generalizations concerning what Hmong Americans consider traditional dress are difficult to make, however three different versions of Hmong American traditional dress eventually emerged from my fieldwork. These three versions sometimes compete for favor within single individuals and certainly among family, gender or age groupings. I refer to the three versions as 'treasure-box traditional dress,' 'old-style traditional dress,' and 'new-style traditional dress.'

Treasure-box traditional ensembles are in most instances worn by women. They are typically composed at least in part of garments that were worn by older relatives in Laos. The faded and less colorful dress is not popular with most teenagers, but limited numbers of women choose to wear the style for special events centered on expression of commitment to tradition and the past. Treasure-box traditional Hmong American ensembles are made up of dress elements consciously selected because they are either old or based upon old prototypes. Treasure-box ensembles were relatively rare at the New Year, but may grow in popularity as more Hmong assimilate into wider American society.

Young women that wear treasure-box traditional ensembles to the New Year tend to come from families which are more assimilated into American culture. The two young women who most strongly endorsed this more conservative version of traditional dress took pride in how successfully their families had integrated into American culture. In contrast to other women I talked to they did not typically attend the New Year wearing traditional dress styles. The year I interviewed them was an exception, as they were part of the stage activities. I was left with the impression that they were dressing for a role, in this case a Teen of the Year contestant, rather than dressing for an individual expression of identity. They felt their positions as Teen of the Year candidates required wearing historically accurate traditional dress. One of these two girls wore a very old-style turban which had been brought from Laos by her mother combined with a Green Hmong skirt with traditional blue batik patterning and red embroidery. Traditional Hmong-style dress, for these girls, is something old and treasured, something associated with the past, to be taken out of the trunks and worn for special occasions.

Old-style traditional ensembles are also worn primarily by women and are generally characterized by relatively conservative use of American trims and accessories and the wearing of styles that have formal recognized linkages with the past. These ensembles feature the wearing of the old-style turban headdress for women. In more innovative old-style ensembles, the dark turbans are adorned with popular new-style turban ties. The headdresses featuring the modern turban tie are a striking synthesis of both the treasure-box traditional and new-style traditional impulses within a single form.

New-style traditional ensembles are generally characterized by openness to American influences and are worn by men as well as women. They are characterized by an openness to American influence in terms of additive trims as well as the wearing of the new-style hat for women. In contrast to the other two styles, new-style traditional Hmong ensembles are an eclectic mix of American and Hmong dress forms. While innovation is limited to decorative trims and reflective surfaces in the old-style traditional ensembles, in the new-style ensembles American dress elements such as gloves, vests, leggings, and suit styles are included.

Teenagers wearing the old-style and new-style traditional ensembles at the New Year generally dress for at least one of the two days of the New Year celebration in Hmong-style dress. In part, because they dress in Hmong-style for the New Year every year, they tend to take pride in having new and innovative versions of traditional dress to display. Those wearing old-style traditional ensembles tend to have lived for a shorter amount of time in the United States. Perhaps the integration of forms of dress into the ensembles happens as the teenagers become more comfortable with the range of American dress forms available. But even within the relative conservative range of adding new trims and new surface designs, these young people find ways to make their largely traditional ensembles appear 'new.' This is in contrast with the attitudes of wearers of treasure-box traditional dress, who shun innovation in any form and look always to the past for validation of their dress as 'traditional.'

Young men and women wearing new-style traditional dress are open to more radical innovation and pride themselves on being trendsetters within the community. As I was interviewing a young man falling into this category, we looked at the ensemble he had recently worn to the New Year. I asked him if he would wear the same clothes next year. His reply expressed that he was committed to having different and new clothes to wear every year and he was confident that his mother would provide him with new designs (AL-M-050). Sure enough, when I saw the young man at the New Year the following year he was wearing a 'new style' of the new-style traditional dress sewn with love by his mother.

The interplay between the teenagers' desire for 'new' new-style traditional dress and the older women who sew their clothes creates a healthy exchange between the two generations. The same young man quoted above captures this generational exchange. In the following comments about his mother, both her grasp of the past and embrace of the present is evident: 'My mother is sort of the cultural bearer. She knows all the stories behind each of the clothing and why we should make it this way and why we should make it that way.' I then commented that his mother, while well versed in traditional dress, seemed very willing to experiment with American fabrics and trims. He answered, 'Yes. She is into fabrics like crazy.' He then went on to argue that his mother was a style trendsetter, that her 'new' New Year's styles always established the latest looks and were often copied by other sewers and designers in the community (AL-M-05).

Individual teenage girls often wear versions of both the old-style and new-style traditional dress to different portions of the two-day New Year celebration. For example one girl who was a contestant in the beauty contest wore the turban with the old-style striped turban tie to the contest because she was expressly requested to dress as traditional as possible:

I wore both [hats and turbans], like in the morning I didn't toss balls or anything, I thought I'd wear it [new-style hat] for the fun of it – so, I wore a hat in the morning because the turban is kind of tight on me and I had to wear it at night too for the contest, so I just wore my hat – I just put it on my head. And then later on when it was almost time to go for my speech, we had to wear our traditional skirts for our speech, so I wore the turban with the stripes [old-style turban tie] because we were supposed to wear our most traditional stuff. (AL-F-01)

In sum, as stage representatives of Hmong American culture, teenagers are sometimes called on to (or choose to) dress in the older-style dress. The same teenager may choose to dress in the new style when they are on the auditorium floor expressing their own individual identity.

The role of dress as a marker of new life and renewal within the annual celebration of the New Year infuses a vitality into Hmong textile arts which continues to enliven the stage and auditorium floor at the New Year. Older Hmong American women still work to create 'new' New Year's dress for their families. These ever new versions of ritual apparel incorporate the old and the new into ever emerging versions of traditional dress. Both old-style and new-style traditional dress remain vitally connected to the past in their embrace of 'newness' in terms of design and decorative detail. The key difference between the two styles is that of the degree of innovative spirit. New-style ensembles not only include new trims, new surface designs, and new fabrics; they also include innovative new forms of dress such as the rooster-style hat and men's vest forms.

In marked contrast, treasure-box traditional dress is a purposeful freezing of tradition in order to maintain historically accurate linkages to the past. This version of traditional dress is purposefully static and unchanging. While ever-changing versions of Hmong traditional dress visibly make sense of being Hmong and American (by combining Hmong and American influences) treasure-box traditional dress is a self-conscious framing of the past.

The three versions of traditional dress send different messages. Old and new-style traditional dress, with their dramatic mix of Hmong American influences, declares: 'We are Hmong – we are American – we are Hmong American.' In contrast, treasure-box traditional dress says, 'Our ancestors were Hmong. We are now American. We will always keep our Hmong heritage in our hearts.' All three versions of traditional dress are visible displays of the Hmong American community's recognition of the value of its cultural past. Old-style and new-style traditional dress, through their blend of American and Hmong cultural elements, are emphatic statements to those outside and inside the community of the need for Hmong American culture to both adapt to American culture and maintain links to the past. Treasure-box traditional ensembles imply that the past is a memory to be treasured and protected. The sentiments expressed are similar to other assimilated groups who pass down traditional garments from one generation to the next out of pride of ethnic heritage.

Dress as a Symbol of Hmong American Ethnicity

Sub-styles of Lao Hmong dress previously described such as Green and White Hmong marked what John Comaroff (1987) would call a totemic boundary line between the related sub-groups. The bounded groups are structurally similar and have roughly the same amount of social and political power. While living in Laos the sub-groups of Hmong spoke different dialects of the same language and performed rituals in slightly different ways. These cultural differences, while internally perceived, were not often not externally noted or appreciated. Dress as a visible sign was more often noticed and commented upon by outsiders, thus perhaps accounting for the use of dress by the outside world, to label the differing sub-groups.

During my first visit to the New Year in November of 1988, I naively assumed that teenagers were wearing distinct sub-styles of dress associated with their family and region of origin. I was thus surprised when a young woman told me to be sure and watch for her the next day as she would be wearing a different ensemble associated with another sub-group. 'And,' she told me, 'you will probably want another picture.' When I interviewed the winner of the 1989 Teen of the Year contest, she proudly showed me photographs of herself wearing four different sub-styles of dress. Young men tend to own fewer sub-styles of dress, but they wear clearly hybrid styles which draw from the range of Hmong sub-styles as well as American dress styles and material culture.

Teenagers I talked to were perplexed by questions concerning why they wore the sub-styles of other groups and generally attributed little meaning to the practice. Most teenagers simply said that it was the style, the American way. But importantly, being a Hmong American rather than a Lao Hmong is often associated with the freedom to wear another subgroup's style. For example, the following is drawn from an interview with a Hmong American female Teen of the Year contestant:

> See that is the change now. Now we can wear any one, any kind. I could be a Green Hmong, I could wear White Hmong clothes, it doesn't really matter. It doesn't really matter in Laos too, but in Laos you wear what you are. But now it is the style. If you like it, you wear it. We are becoming Americanized in that way. (AL-F-01)

It is typical that the teenagers discuss the impulse to wear the other styles as a fashion impulse or as an aesthetic choice; 'it looks good,' 'it is the new style' are very often the words used by the teenagers. The following response is addressed to the mixing of the sub-styles within a single ensemble: 'I usually mix them up. I wear the hat with the White, and the hat doesn't go with the White dress, it doesn't really matter but it surely looks good, so why not?' (AL-F-05)

The practice of mixing the sub-styles together and wearing the sub-styles of other groups is documented throughout the country. Writing on research conducted in Philadelphia, Sally Peterson comments that 'there are not many Green Hmong families in Philadelphia [an Eastern Hmong American community], but almost every family with daughters owns a Green Hmong skirt, particularly if it is made in the new style' (1990: 94). Using fieldwork in Montana, a Rocky Mountain Hmong American community, Susan Lindbergh compares how teenage Hmong American girls dress for the New Year with the way their mothers dress in Laos:

> Transition is evident in the costumes that the girls wear . . . Whereas their mothers dressed for the New Year's . . . depending upon the sub-group into which they were born, the young women in this study each own costumes representative of at least two, if not three, different sub-groups from which they select to wear, depending upon personal preference. Wealthy girls may wear a different costume for each night of the New Year celebration to display their riches. Frequently sub-group garments are mixed, creating a hybrid costume.(1990: 45)

In a similar vein, Joanne Cubbs (1986) reported that new-style ensembles worn by teenagers at the New Year in Sheboygan, Wisconsin, another Midwestern Hmong American community, combine elements of White Hmong and Green Hmong dress(71).

While most wearers tie forms of new-style dress worn to the St Paul New Year to Lao Hmong prototypes, the popular rooster-style women's New Year hat is consistently classified as Hmong American. This is despite evidence, as noted in Chapter 4, that similar hat styles did exist in historical Green Hmong Dress (Peterson 1990; AL-F-03). Early versions of the American-style New Year hat combined White Hmong handwork with a Green Hmong children's hat style. The dramatic mixing of the two major sub-styles of dress within a single form makes the hat a premiere example of dress that is expressive of a cohesive Hmong identity. The contemporary versions of the rooster-style hat have integrated elements of American material culture into the design as well. Sequins, lace, and American trims have been borrowed and creatively integrated into striking symbols of being Hmong, being American, being Hmong American.

The Hmong, like the immigrant groups cited by Sarna (1978), entered the Thai refugee camps, and later the United States as a fragmented group of refugees continuing to categorize themselves by what Comaroff (1987) would label a totemic classification. Individuals became more intensely conscious of their *ethnic*, as opposed to *totemic*, identities as the integrity of their world was threatened by outside forces. While allegiance to the White or Green Hmong sub-group or to a specific clan was of fundamental importance in the Lao village context, it became progressively less important as the Hmong were challenged and discriminated against on the basis of their more inclusive ethnic identity. Sarna (1978) posits that as cultural groups endure discrimination based upon an externally ascribed ethnic boundary line, that line becomes more important internally as well. When the Lao Hmong were targeted for extermination by the communists, based upon their ethnic rather than totemic identity, their ethnic identity became of critical significance. As they moved into refugee camps and relocated to the United States, they continued to be treated as a cohesive ethnic group and received both positive and negative treatment based upon that identity. It became an identity they could use as a tool to gain support for higher education, welfare benefits, and other forms of relocation assistance while at the same time it was used as a basis for discrimination.

Within the urban Midwestern community in which I did my research, Hmong American teenagers experienced a higher degree of discrimination based on their ethnic identity than did the adult members of their families. Many adults live daily lives centered almost exclusively within Hmong American neighborhoods or housing complexes, whereas adolescents are forced into more direct contact with the larger American society within the public school system. Aside from the obvious biological characteristics of appearance differentiating the Hmong from white and black students, they are also ascribed a strong separate identity by other, more successful, Southeast Asian groups, particularly the Vietnamese (Baizerman and Hendricks 1988). Thus, Hmong youth are more forcefully compelled to accept the validity of their ascribed identity because that identity affects their everyday lives.

Using Sarna's (1978) work on American ethnicity, the transformation of regional sub-styles of Lao Hmong dress into a cohesive Hmong American style may be interpreted as symbolic of Hmong American ethnicity. Teenagers, as the generation most acutely experiencing discrimination based on their ascribed ethnic identity, wear New Year's dress which expresses Hmong cohesiveness and pride. By wearing a mix of Hmong sub-styles, teenagers visibly accept and celebrate their ascribed ethnic identity both as individuals and as corporate representatives of their families and communities.

Clear gender differences exist in the way that ethnic identity is expressed. As discussed in the previous chapters, young men feel much more compelled to dress in styles which express versions of American success than do their female peers. A majority of new-style traditional dress worn by young men to the New Year is based on Euro-American business suit styles with variations in cut, surface design choices, and accessories influenced by Lao Hmong menswear styles. In contrast, young women dress to express their role in the community as bearers of culture. It is women, not the men, who wear the strongest symbol of unchanging tradition, treasure-box traditional dress. However, in all three styles of women's traditional dress (treasure-box, old-style, and new-style), basic elements drawn from Lao Hmong styles have been largely retained. One example is the Green Hmong skirts, which wrap the waist in a heavy layer of cloth. These symbols of past gender roles emphasizing fecundity continue to be an important part of a majority of the dress observed at the New Year.

Another indication of the association of women's dress with the past is the high degree of conflict related to women's headdress choices. In the face of rapid change related to relocation to the United States, the turban emerged as a symbol of enduring tradition. As in many other instances of cultural contact, women dress to tether the community to the past, whereas men dress to express the ability to lead the community into the future. Given this role, women's lives in the Hmong community are deeply affected by trying to balance the desire to remain true to traditional life and values with the need to be accepted and succeed in the United States.

Interpretations posed in this section of the book vividly illustrate the formative role of dress within the ritual context. In the Hmong American community, dress does not simply reflect a cultural world, it is helping formulate a cultural world. As a public display of what it means to be a Hmong American male or female, New Year's dress is a flexible and expressive medium. As an aspect of material culture, it expresses the central debates threatening the cohesiveness of the community. Dress used within ritual performances offers the opportunity to observe and capture culture in the making. These Hmong examples complement and illustrate Victor Turner's (1988) work on ritual as performance by moving material culture and its transformation into the ritual arena. As argued by Turner and his followers, and visibly brought to life at the New Year, 'cultural change, cultural continuity, and cultural transmission' (Bruner 1986: 12) all occur within the context of the New Year and are expressed through the dressed and evaluated body. As the past is brought to life through ritual re-enactment, so too it is reinterpreted in light of present concerns and realities, in a visible display of what it means to Hmong in America.

6

African American Debutante Balls: Presenting Women of Quality

As a white mother of two daughters and a product of the populist American Midwest, I was at first ambivalent about doing research on African American debutante balls. My confusion grew as I met with and talked to the mothers and female community leaders who helped support and organize the balls. The black women I met who were involved in planning the event were strong, outspoken and generous; caring deeply about people at all income levels within their community. As mothers they wanted their daughters to succeed and thrive both professionally and personally. 'Why?' I kept asking myself, 'would these women choose to develop a debutante ball?' In my mind the idea of a debutante ball conjured up the negative image of girls bedecked in finery and shopping for a husband. The class-based history of white debutante balls coupled with their traditional focus on courtship and marriage at first seemed in conflict with the assertive competence I sensed in the black women I met and talked to at the beginning of the project. As a white feminist raised on the rhetoric of the mainstream women's movement, a debutante ball was far from what I myself would hope for my own daughters – maybe a basketball league, or a reading group, or a theatre production, but a debutante ball? With these conflicting feelings I began fieldwork on a ritual I both came to understand and appreciate.

History of Public Venues for the Display of African American Women's Dress

The concept of reconstruction is a primary theme expressed in African American dress and culture. Henry Louis Gates (1988) uses the term when he observes that American 'blacks seem to have felt the need to "reconstruct" their image to whites probably since the dreadful day in 1619 when the first boatload of us disembarked in Virginia' (13). Stripped of clothing, family networks, social customs, and ties to land and heritage, Africans were turned into owned property and were denied their own identity and history when they entered the United States. African men, women, and children summarily lost control of their bodies, their appearance, and their identities. The road back to self-identification has been difficult and central to understanding African American expressive culture and experience.[1]

The debutante balls thus must be interpreted as a part of a long history of African Americans using dress within public venues to display reconstructed versions of gendered identity. Severed from their cultural past and denied many other means of expressing themselves, Africans brought into slavery in America quickly turned to their bodies to display pride and cultural values (Foster 1997). During the slavery period black women presented themselves for public display at the weekly church services. Daily work styles were plain, but women dressed up themselves and their families specially for Sunday worship. West African textile traditions were drawn from by women as they crafted and put together creative African and American ensembles. WPA interviews reviewed by Shane and Graham White (1998) indicate that black female slaves were able to achieve a full range of colors using natural dyes and that they were weaving using techniques brought over with them from Africa. Strip weaving, traditionally the domain of men in West Africa,[2] became a part of women's work in America, likely due to American division of labor patterns (Wahlman 1993: 21).

Aesthetic expression through dress and appearance was a ready means for African Americans to reformulate cultural definitions of male and female gender on the American continent. Though attempts were made to curtail black slaves' ability to express themselves through appearance, both black men and women quickly found ways to defy the formal and informal statutes limiting their personal style (Foster 1997). A distinct African American style began to develop early in the slave period that drew from the patterns of clothing use and aesthetic principles drawn from West Africa but also making creative use of American dress forms. The notion that black Africans reworked rather than simply retained aspects of West African dress and

1. The uplift movement of the turn of the twentieth century is important background to understanding the African American struggle for self-identification. Kevin Gaines' (1996) book is a good source of information on this movement.

2. The summer I spent in Nigeria (1995) I observed many women weaving strip cloth. This is a new phenomenon and apparently is spurred by entrepreneurs primarily interested in making money weaving the popular cloth. Women traditionally weave wider cloth, which is currently not as marketable in Nigeria.

aesthetic attitudes is stressed by Kobena Mercer, and is an accepted tenet of my thinking as well. Mercer argues that:

> our attention must now be directed not so much to the retention of actual artifacts but to the reworking of what may be seen as a 'neo-African' approach to the aesthetic in disaporean cultural formations. The patterns and practices of aesthetic stylization developed by black cultures in First World societies may be seen as modalities of cultural practices inscribed in critical engagement with the dominant white culture and at the same time expressive of a 'neo-African' approach to the pleasures of beauty at the level of everyday life. (1990: 257)

What is critical in Mercer's approach is the emphasis upon the creative vitality of African American expressive culture that results from the interplay between West African aesthetic attitudes posed in a not always easy relationship with mainstream America. What results is neither 'African' nor 'American,' but rather a creative fusion that reflects the resilient pride of West Africans displaced then reconstructed in an American context.

While weaving and dyeing in traditional styles directly affected some expressive material culture, for example African American quilts (see Wahlman 1993), the impact on clothing tends to be expressed more in terms of preferences and artistic choices emanating from a synergetic fusion of West African aesthetic canons and American culture. Female slaves were often charged with the role of translating hand-me-downs and spare pieces of cloth into dress styles expressing African American identity. The concept and salience of black style emerged early in African American history, and women's handwork was often used to embellish or modify the limited range of apparel available to slaves to better fit emerging African American aesthetic preferences. Slaves living in urban settings in the 1850s organized formal balls modeled on balls given by their white owners. These balls were an early venue for display of black women's dress. Accounts of the period indicate that black female slaves wore showy eclectic styles and ornate hats to the balls. A white visitor to a Charleston, South Carolina ball in 1853 commented:

> The striking features of Negro evening dress consisted in astonishing turbans with marabou feathers, into which added accessories of squib shape and other forms were inserted. (Hazzard-Gordon 1990: 51)

A black woman that grew up in the late years of the Civil War and early reconstruction period remembered that even patching and darning was done in a 'stylish' manner (White and White 1998: 22). In the rare event that blacks were given new clothing, they often found reasons to modify it to their own taste. For example, a white teacher during the reconstruction period expressed dismay when her newly freed black female students took dresses she gave them home and added on 'the most unsuitable material, putting old cloth with the new, and a cotton frill to a worsted skirt' (White and White 1998: 23), thus translating the dresses from the white world into their own idiom.

As freed slaves moved into northern cities public venues were limited, with church services remaining an important arena for expression of African American female identity. Attempts to create public social settings for blacks in the early 1800s were often stymied by interference from the surrounding white populations who quickly managed to shut down tea and ice cream parlors catering to black customers. Many urban blacks took the streets as a means of socializing and display during this period (White and White 1998).

Free African American women living in New York in 1832 were noticed for their stylish attire and were described by visitors as being 'in the height of fashion' (White and White 1998: 91). However comments from the period indicate that black women enacted a version of fashionability that included stronger contrasts in color and pattern than were customary. Shane and Graham White suggest that newly freed slaves living in cities in the North continued to be influenced by aesthetic preferences emanating out of the West African past:

> We would suggest that the newly liberated blacks deliberately, consciously, and publicly tested the boundaries of freedom. At an individual level the result was a venturing out into the city streets by African Americans garbed in colorful and, what often seemed to whites, bizarre combinations of clothes–ensembles that reflect the existence of an African American aesthetic. (1998: 94)

In addition, and important to this investigation, was the creation of the first African American formal balls in the Eastern cities. While these balls were modeled on white prototypes, they were also reinterpreted to reflect the lives and cultural backgrounds of African Americans. White and White (1998) point out the African American composers modified the European dance music to incorporate West African rhythms and at least in one case decorations for the ball included images of Africa (1998: 100). The early black balls apparently made fun of the exclusivity that characterized the white formal balls, as in jest ball organizers in Philadelphia in 1828 told ticket distributors to 'furnish no person with tickets who could not trace his pedigree as far back as his mother, at the least' (White and White 1998: 102).

In the first three decades of the twentieth century, Jim Crow as an institution dramatically impacted the venues and freedom of black Americans (Gaines 1996; White and White 1998). Subservience as an attitude was expected of blacks and those who challenged white supremacy often suffered for their transgressions. African American styles of dress and movement were also curbed during this period, but blacks found safe venues for personal expression in their churches and in the streets of their neighborhoods. The church was a place where black women's moral character, beauty, and style was openly recognized and appreciated. At church a black woman could walk down the aisle holding her head up high topped with a fancy and heavily decorated hat and wearing a style that reflected her African American heritage. White observers to the dress of black churchgoers continued to notice differences between their own dress choices and those made by African Americans:

> As in slavery times, the aggressive color combinations preferred by blacks attracted whites' attention. 'African Americans,' [commented] Willa Johnson [a white Mississippi woman], showed a 'decided taste for vivid colors' so that, 'without hesitation, green, yellow, and red are clashed together' and a 'wild colored sash' was often added for effect. (White and White 1998: 175)

Urban streets in black neighborhoods also became important showcases for black women's style as men often strolled their female companions through the rich mix of music and fashion that enlivened black city street life during this period. Famous city streets such as Beale Street in Memphis became a part of black history and myth (White and White 1998).

Despite the dampening effect of Jim Crow, particularly in the South, the emergence of democratized fashion and beauty aids, the rise of an ideal of beauty centered on modernity, and the development and popularity of jazz as a musical form all combined in the second decade of the twentieth century to create venues for black female style that began to attract attention nationally as well as internationally. Beginning in the 1920s, African American newspapers and other publications began featuring African American women. In part this was related to an effort on the part of middle-class blacks of influence to combat stereotypes through the conscious reconstruction of black female identity for those inside and outside the community, but it was also a pure celebration of African American female beauty, style and accomplishment. Black women's intellectual and social accomplishments were stressed as well as their beauty (White and White 1998).

Black female beauty was also being displayed on stage in both Europe and the United States as many Europeans and white Americans became fascinated voyeurs of black culture. Stage shows in the United States directed toward a white audience tended to feature lighter-skinned black women with Euro-American features. In Europe fascination with African culture among artists and writers resulted in a more open embrace of black American culture and art. African American writers, performers, and musicians found a ready and appreciative audience in Europe and many chose to live abroad. Stage shows in Europe also featured black women where they were presented as inspirational embodiments of an exotic African world view. Josephine Baker, an African American dancer of the era, was extremely popular in France where she made blatant connections to African culture a staple of her performance. While some argue that these performances reinforced compromising female gender constructions for blacks, I would argue that by bringing black beauty out of the closet and on stage to white as well as black audiences, they played a significant role in initiating a movement that will culminate in wider appreciation for black beauty and arts both in Europe and the United States.

Fashion became democratized in the 1920s. Information on fashion trends was spreading across the country via department stores, newspapers, and magazines. Department stores, as an important public space for American women, grew in popularity and importance during this time period. Black women, excluded from this public domain by segregation policies of the period, also found venues for taking part in the national trend toward fashionable dress and behavior. African American fashion reviews became common throughout the United States in the 1920s and 1930s. Models featured in the reviews reflected a broad range of black female beauty and contrasted with the stage shows directed toward white American audiences with their bias toward African American women with more Euro-American features (White and White 1998: 218).

Fashion reviews were sponsored and organized by the growing black middleclass in cities throughout the United States as a way of displaying the strength and leadership within their ranks (White and White 1998: 213). At the same time these reviews delineated growing class boundaries between blacks living in major urban centers. Similarly, the early African American debutante balls held within these communities, most often sponsored by African American professional men's associations, helped mark class boundaries as well as spotlighting the beauty, grace, and character of the daughters of prominent African American families.

African American Debutante Balls

Debutante balls were first held in Europe during a period of growing class-consciousness in the seventeenth century. Upper-class Europeans, anxious to maintain their hold on social exclusivity, used the balls to underscore the importance of heredity in determining status and protect themselves against a growing middle class. Women of marriageable age were carefully presented to a select audience of suitors by their families, thus encouraging marriage within the ranks of the established aristocracy. The tradition spread to the United States through the monied elite of New York, where they were used to maintain class distinctions as the nouveau riche attempted to integrate into the ranks of old monied families at the end of the nineteenth and beginning of the twentieth century. Social standing as well as wealth traditionally determined the ability of a young woman to participate in these exclusive rites of passage.

According to Katrina Hazzard-Gordon (1990) African American debutante balls emerged in cities in the post-emancipation period for several reasons. Firstly, the balls were an outgrowth of the more broadly based uplift movement. The African American uplift movement was led by the black urban elite and emerged as a means of raising the quality of life for all free blacks through education and social actions.[3] The balls were sponsored by newly formed voluntary associations in an effort to 'demonstrate that blacks were worthy of the American dream' (163). They also served a fund-raising function, with money being used for causes related to racial uplift. Finally, the balls were staged as venues for young black women who were excluded from participating in white balls of the period (163–4).

The early roots of the ball within the ranks of the black elite affected the attitudes of many blacks toward the events. E. Franklin Frazier (1962), writing about the events in the 1950s and 1960s, interprets the balls as indulgent expressions of upper-class blacks' need for recognition. He points out that the balls were more show than substance and that many of the participants' families were financially drained by the extravagance. Frazier, and many of his black contemporaries, viewed the balls as derivative of white upper-class social functions and imitative of the behavior and values of 'white' society. Using the Cleveland, Ohio cotillion as a point of reference, contemporary writer Katrina Hazzard-Gordon argues that the continued traditions of the balls 'encourage and objectify class division in the black community' (1990: 171). She cites prohibitive cost as well as class barriers to participation of middle- and lower-class black women in the events.

---

3. Black leadership within the uplift movement was divided between W.E.B. Du Bois, of the integrationist school of thought and Booker T. Washington, of the accommodationist school of thought (Gates and West 1996: 33). Du Bois was an American-style optimist who called for uplift through education, followed by political and social change. In contrast, Washington led blacks in a more politically and socially conservative direction staying safely within existing white political and social structures.

The cotillion in Waterloo, Iowa that I researched contrasts markedly with the balls described by Hazzard-Gordon. The Waterloo, Iowa ball was organized in 1986 by female leaders within the community to support and honor young women entering into adulthood. The patriarchal roots of the older balls with their emphasis upon presenting well-born daughters of men with high social standing does not resonate within this event. Instead I was struck by the strength of the black women within the community reaching out to support other younger black women. The ball is organized by Club Les Dames, an organization of African American women with a strong commitment to supporting the success of young black women. The ball is the primary event the organization sponsors each year. Female organizers stress that the ball functions to display the social and academic accomplishments of young African American women. In one organizer's words, 'The ball focuses on the academic and positive things young women have done' (Abebe 1995). The profits from the sale of tickets to the ball are used to sponsor a scholarship fund.

Contemporary African American debutante balls in this region of the United States have moved in the direction of stressing the academic accomplishments and community service records of the participants, rather than their social standing. To minimize the impact of socio-economic background of the event, many sponsoring organizations provide scholarships or economic assistance for needy young women. The ball I researched has participation requirements and expectations that allow young women from a wide range of social and economic backgrounds to attend and be presented as debutantes. Debutante candidates are required to be in academic good standing and involved in community service activities. Young women who are pregnant or who have already given birth to a child are excluded from participation. Tickets to the event are relatively inexpensive (under ten dollars) and unlike the balls described by Hazzard-Gordon families of the girls I interviewed did not rent hotel rooms or plan lavish dinner parties as a part of the social event. Former debutantes gave me estimates of participation costs ranging from $250 to $600, depending largely on the cost of their dress, which is the most expensive item in the debutante's budget.

Debutantes are recruited both informally by Club Les Dames members and through a systematic mailing sent to all young black women who are seniors in the local high schools. Young women who meet the requirements for participation and are interested request and fill out an application, along with a minimal fee. Not all the women living in the community are interested in being a part of the event, so not all eligible young women choose to participate. Former debutantes told me that some young black women, particularly athletes, were not attracted to the event and therefore chose not to apply to be debutantes. Those young women that make a commitment to become debutantes enter into a series of classes preparing them to enter the world as debutantes. While one of the classes is devoted to etiquette, in some years classes have included sessions on spirituality and goal setting. In addition to the formal ball debutantes and their mothers also participate in a mid-winter Mother-Daughter Tea.

Reasons for participation vary, but most young debutantes talked about the importance of the event within the community and to their families. Unlike class-based and extremely formal debutante balls, the African American balls I attended are family and community affairs that draw audience members from all ranks of the African American community. For the first nine years the event was held at a ballroom that served a range of community functions including the annual black fashion show, benefit concerts, and anniversary and wedding dances. For the past four years the balls has been held in the ballroom at the downtown convention center, a location that debutantes and organizers feel lends more elegance and decorum to the event. The low ticket costs result in a large African American audience, however I was only one of a handful of audience members from outside of the black community.

Dress styles worn by the debutantes are typical representations of bridal fashions of the current season. Young debs and their mothers typically buy the dresses from local bridal shops or have them sewn by black women within the community who are known for their sewing skills. Dresses are full length white gowns and generally feature a fitted bodice, full skirt, and natural waistline (see Figure 6.1). Young women generally have their hair professionally styled for the event, and typical coiffures are formal French roll styles, often with ringlets (see Figure 6.2). The culminating effect is bride-like, in fact it is not unusual for a debutante to wear her dress for her wedding later on in her life. Young women range in body type and appearance, reflecting that participation in the event is not based on conformation to rigid ideals of physical beauty. Varieties of black beauty are presented and celebrated by the event and young women's accomplishments range from athletic ability to academic performance. Male escorts and presenters dress in formal black tuxedos, thus underscoring the wedding-like appearance of the participants at this coming-of-age ceremony. Mothers tend to dress in evening wear for the event.

While dress at the ball is formal for participants, family members, and organizers, the atmosphere is easy-going and comfortable. Audience members who do not have roles in the event dress in varying levels of formality and use the event as a means of socializing in a relatively casual way with friends and family. The audience is seated in folding chairs around round banquet tables in groupings of family and friends. Debutantes and their families are

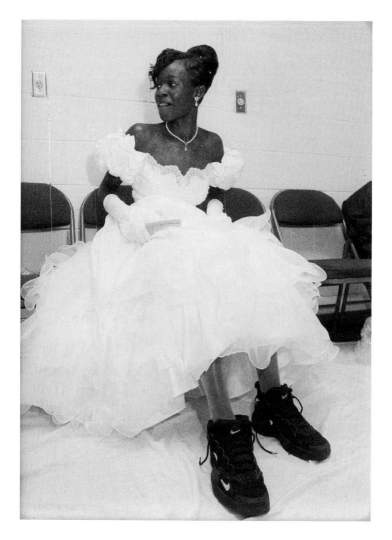

Figure 6.1. African American Debutante in gown and Nikes. Photography, *Waterloo Courier*.

seated in front-row tables surrounding the stage. A small amount of dance floor is reserved surrounding the stage for debutantes to waltz with their presenters and escorts. The larger dance floor is off to the side of the room and the music is provided by a disc jockey. The event has the feel of a large extended family gathering, with lots of side conversations, children, and good humor. It is significant that children as well as adults feel comfortable and welcome within the ballroom and on the dance floor.

Figure 6.2. Debutantes dressing for the ball. Photograph, *Waterloo Courier*.

The structure of the event blends aspects of an American-style beauty contest, a fashion show, a social dance, and a wedding ceremony, and follows closely the precedents set by white ball organizers (Haynes 1998: 53). The young debutante's name is announced from the stage as she enters and walks across the stage. As the candidate walks alone down a runway similar to those used in fashion shows a female announcer and member of Club Les Dames lists her school and community activities, reads a favorite quotation, and tells about who the girl considers her most important personal mentor. The young woman is presented to the community by her father or other male surrogate who meets her at the end of the runway and takes her hand to help her down the steps. Her mother then walks up and hugs the debutante and the three walk to a table designated for the debutante and her entourage. After the presentation of all the debutantes, the young women are all led to the dance floor by their presenters. After a brief moment of preparation the formal opening waltz for the debutante begins as she is led around the dance floor by her male presenter.

Following the waltz, debutantes and their presenters return to their tables and escorts are formally and individually introduced to the audience. Similar to the young women, male escorts are given formal dress guidelines that are followed. Young men wear black formal suits and appear 'spruced up' for the affair. Despite the formal black uniformity of dress, young male escorts express their own distinct style through coiffure, body movement, and gait. Escorts strut, preen, and play with the audience as they are introduced. Many use long stem roses as props hiding them in sleeves and behind their backs as they walk from the back of the stage to the front of the room to receive the hand of the debutante. In contrast with the respectful silence of the audience during the presentation of the debutantes, the gestures and panache of the escorts often draws appreciative laughter and sometimes cheers from the audience.

After their introduction the escorts walk to the table of the debutante they escorted and typically present the young woman with flowers. Respect is also paid to the family and the debutante through a stylized bow. The father or male surrogate then formally turns over the debutante to her escort who is seated with the family as the other escorts are introduced. After all the escorts are seated, the debutantes are once again led to the front formal dance floor to waltz with their escorts. Presenters and mothers join the young couples on the dance floor and the young debutante waltz's her first waltz as a newly presented debutante. This formal waltz closes the stage program and the remainder of the evening is an open dance with popular music provided by the disc jockey. Formality is dropped for this part of the evening and children, teenagers, and adults all join the debutantes and escorts on the dance floor.

The Debutante Cotillion Ball as Ritual: Interpretive Analysis

Club Les Dames organizers stress that the ball is an opportunity for a positive portrayal of black women 'in a society where they aren't always portrayed positively' (Abebe 1995). This comment indicating that the ideal presented within the ball is a part of a purposeful attempt on the part of the older organizers to reconstruct images of black women through a public event featuring young black women of integrity and promise. Historical stereotypes depicting black women as promiscuous and lacking in intelligence and grace are confronted within this ritual by a public presentation of young women of scholastic merit wearing quintessential symbols of purity, white formal dresses.

The selective nature of this version of a coming-of-age ritual makes it slightly different than many others, in that the number of participants is narrowed to those considered the most promising within the community. Following after the model of uplift espoused by W.E.B. Du Bois, higher education is raised up as the means for this select number of young female high school graduates to advance to positions of prominence and leadership in the community. Social standing is not emphasized in the Waterloo Ball. Instead, accomplishments of young debutantes are highlighted including academic honors, involvement in extracurricular activities, and future college or university plans.

The social and popular nature of the balls underscores their inspirational role within the community. Many of the debutantes I interviewed had attended the ball as girls or young teenagers and worked hard in school and within the community in order to become debutantes as high school seniors. The ritual causes self-reflection among older women in the audience as well, as they assess their own lives in comparison to the young women being presented as exemplar. One of my college students, a black woman who had gotten pregnant in high school and was thus not eligible to be a debutante, sat with me one year at the ball and talked to me about her struggles for education as a single parent of a young child. In this sense the ritual is a means of bringing problems to the surface for reflection, discussion, and perhaps internal or corporate resolution. While only a fraction of young women in the community are presented as debutantes, larger numbers are affected through audience participation as well as more general community response to the event.

A key theme that emerges from the balls is the importance of the mother-daughter bond within the Waterloo African American community. The salience of this relationship struck me early in my research as I ate lunch with a Club Les Dames member whose daughter was a recent debutante. I was struck by the emphasis she placed upon establishing a strong relationship with her daughter during her senior year in preparation for the separation that would occur during her years at college. As this mother described the year-long debutante process, including classes and teas and purchasing the ball dress, it was clear that an important function of the ball was to draw mothers and daughters together at the point where the young women were leaving their childhood homes and becoming independent women. In this sense the ball truly functions as a rite of passage for these young women, as they are mentored by both women within the community and their families at the juncture in their lives when they are entering into adulthood.

The importance of bonds between older and younger women in the black community is also expressed in the responses debutantes give to questions concerning adults who they have been affected by and admire. One of the questions all debutantes are asked to answer is 'Who do you admire most?' The most frequent answer is a female relative, typically a mother or grand-mother. One can feel the strength these young women gain from their mothers and grandmothers in the written answers published in the Cotillion programs.

Two answers that are typical follow: my mother is my most admired person because 'she is a strong educated black woman' and my most admired person is 'My mom, because in spite of all her setbacks, she still remains as composed and confident as ever. She also has always kept her trust in God no matter what the problem was' (Club Les Dames 1997). References to being guided by Christian faith and by female members of the family are strong themes within the Cotillion Balls and ring true with the history of black women using their Christian faith as a means of overcoming adversity and inspiring their children to higher goals and right living.

Turner's concept of ritual as an arena wherein conflicts and problems are articulated and solutions posed is helpful in interpreting the evolution of the Cotillion Ball from a male-sponsored class-based event, to a female-sponsored event focused strongly upon mother-daughter relationships. Black mothers trying to raise American daughters have found the passageway between childhood and adulthood difficult dating back to the slavery period. During the time of slavery, black mothers took particular care to try to protect their daughters from becoming sexually involved with white owners and their sons. Temptations for developing relationships with white men were great during this period as workloads and additional rations were often given to coopera-tive female slaves. In addition some children born from mixed white/black unions were given advantages and sometimes sent north as free blacks. As a defense to this pattern of abusing young female slaves mothers developed moral codes they tried hard to communicate to their daughters.

Problems between young black women and their white employers continued even after emancipation. At the World Columbian Exposition in 1893, one of the first opportunities for black women to address an interracial audience on women's issues, black women expressed their outrage that their daughters working as domestic workers were being sexually harassed by their white male employers (Giddings 1984: 86–7). In the contemporary period, the Anita Hill hearings brought forward many of the same feelings as black women wrote essays in response to this national controversy. In one essay written by a black woman she recalls her mother's attempts to protect her honor and virtue as she was growing up in the 1950s:

Many black women today will recall how their mothers, in response to impro-prieties, and because young African American females were so widely perceived as both vulnerable and sexually available, often acted on the assumption that the only way to protect their daughter's virtue was to repress even healthy expressions of independence and sexuality. These women, my own mother among them, insisted that the girls return home earlier at night than white girls, and wear less revealing clothes and less make-up and jewelry (no pierced ears, please, and certainly no ankle bracelets), lest they be considered provocative, accessible, and compliant sexual targets. (Alexander 1995: 13)

The clothes worn by the young black women at the debutante ball align them with generations of white women whose virtue was recognized and protected. While at the same time the balls speak to the intellectual and spiritual potential of the participants. When seen as a whole the event validates and supports these young women as they enter adulthood and bonds them to generations of black women that have fought hard to provide safe and supportive havens for their developing daughters.

In sum, the Club Les Dames Debutante Ball, and classes that proceed the event, provide a formal means for mothers to guide their daughters consciously through a process of self-reflection and planning. While debutantes and their mothers are most intensely affected by the ritual, the entire community is given public space to focus upon and recognize the integrity and leadership potential of these young black women. Over time I came to better understand and appreciate black female leaders' commitment to the tradition of African American debutante balls. The issues I face as a white mother of two daughters are different than those confronting black mothers in my community. The history of young black women is a legacy of compromise and imposed identity that the public rituals I witnessed addressed and to some extent resolved. By presenting this select group of young black female debutantes as valuable, virtuous, and exemplar American women, Club Les Dames had a wider effect of helping many women sense their own potential and value.

The fact that the debutante ball is a communal public event is significant. Ritual, as an arena wherein conflict is expressed, debated, and to some extent resolved has been used since slavery times to reconstruct black womanhood. Ritualized excuses to dress, such as promenades to church, formalized strolls down the avenue, fashion parades, and beauty contests, were all public enactments that contributed to the development of images of black women that challenged cultural stereotypes and helped women recognize their own potential and receive the respect of others.

7

'It was Style, with a Capital "S"' Versions of Being Male Presented at the Beautillion Ball

> The first male image that I carry is not of my father but of a friend and neighbor, Charlie Burley, the brilliant Hall of Fame prizefighter. A combination of intelligence, the handsome yet bruised face, the swollen knuckles embodying the speed and power and grace of his rough trade. The starched white shirt, the embossed silk tie, the cashmere coat, the exquisite felt fur of the broad-rimmed quintessential hundred-dollar Stetson (the kind Staggerlee wore), and the highly polished yam-colored Florsheim shoes that completed his Friday night regalia. It was style with a capital 'S'. But it was more than being a connoisseur of fine haberdashery; it was attitude and presentation. The men on the corner with their big hats and polished shoes carried and lent a weight to a world that was beholden to their casual elegance as they mocked the condition of their life and paraded through the streets like warrior kings. (Wilson 1995: xi)

'Style,' it is with this image of a black man that August Wilson chooses to open his foreword to Don Belton's (1995) compilation of essays by black men writing on masculinity. Bouncing off that image are the words of my white teenage daughter walking in the kitchen after school talking about the walk and talk of the lone black male in her junior high English class who far outshines his white peers in mode of presentation. 'He is "hot",' she declares, and goes on to describe his walk, talk, and demeanor. Rollin' back the clock, I remember my first year at the Beautillion Ball. All the Beautillion candidates are dressed in simple formal black, but one black beau raised the roof with his walk, his look, and his coiffure. 'Why,' I early asked myself, does male style mean so much within the African American community?

Writers on America popular culture and the African American experience have noted the importance and impact of black style on American expressive culture. In particular documentation of the black power movement of the

1960s focused attention upon the role of black style in defining black identity and in affecting national consciousness. From Tom Wolfe's (1970) scathing portraits of the New York liberal elite entertaining the Black Panthers in politically correct salons in the 1960s to William Van DeBurg's (1992) academic analysis of the role of black style in African American self-actualization, scholars and writers have noted the internal importance of appearance to black males and the impact of their deportment and style on wider American culture (see also Mercer 1990 and Kelley 1994).

From the beginning of the black power movement the relationship between appearance and maintenance of cultural integrity and heritage has been stressed in the black community. Barbara Ann Teer, writing in 1968 and quoted by Van DeBurg (1992) stated:

> The way we talk (the rhythms of our speech which naturally fit our impulses), the way we walk, sing, dance, pray, laugh, eat, make love, and finally, *most important* [my emphasis], the way we look, makes up our cultural heritage. There is nothing like it or equal to it, it stands alone in comparison to other cultures. It is uniquely, beautifully, personally ours and no one can emulate it. (Van DeBurg 1992: 192)

It is within this context that the dress and deportment styles of the young beaux must be interpreted and understood. Appearance isn't simply an expression of identity for these young men, it is a formative medium used to create and sustain African American identity and culture.

Overview and Description: Young Gentlemen's Beautillion

The Beautillion Ball in the Iowa community in which I did my research was an outgrowth of the women's Cotillion. Male organizers stressed that they wanted to develop a male version of the coming-of-age ball because they felt the debutante Cotillion Ball had successfully raised self-esteem and aspirations of many young women in the African American community. The first Young Gentlemen's Beautillion Ball in the community was held in 1995. I attended balls in 1996, 1997, and 1998. The balls are held in a large downtown convention center the weekend of graduation for the local high schools and were positioned in the community as events honoring outstanding black graduates. Similar male balls also emerged at about the same time period in Detroit, Michigan and Davenport, Iowa, both Midwestern American cities with large African American populations. Therefore this case-study could be interpreted within a larger context of trends within African American communities in this region of the United States.

The sponsoring organization for the Young Gentlemen's Beautillion in Waterloo, Iowa is an African American men's professional organization entitled The Black Alliance. The mission of the men's organization reproduced below is linked to W.E B. Du Bois' concept of uplift through education and leadership:

> The Mission of The Black Alliance is to *uplift* [my emphasis], strengthen, and educate our African-American community through positive interaction. We are an organization whose members are socially conscientious individuals whose goals and aims are towards the betterment of our African-American community.

The structure of the organization is modeled on business rather than social organizations, with a Chief Executive Officer (CEO) and Chairman heading the organization and a President. In addition to the Beautillion Ball, The Black Alliance sponsors economic workshops in the community, provides school supplies for black children, and organizes youth activities such as trips to major league baseball games and campouts. At the 1996 Beautillion Ball all twenty-one of the members of the Black Alliance were brought on stage with introductions including place of employment. All members had a strong history of involvement in the Waterloo black community and had jobs indicating middle and upper-middle-class positions within the community.

The Young Gentlemen's Beautillion Ball, like the women's Cotillion Ball, is the final stage of a mentoring process between black youth and prominent (same-sex) adults in the African American community. In contrast to the women's mentoring process, which is more etiquette-based, The Black Alliance emphasizes professional job-related mentoring in an effort to encourage the young men toward setting career goals. Similar to young debutantes, young black men are chosen to participate in the ball on the basis of academic standing and involvement in school and community activities. African American athletes, who are often the recipients of college athletic scholarships, are the clear favorites of the audience at some balls. However generalizations are difficult as in 1998 a young man with an extremely strong record of community service and minimal participation in athletics was the most roundly applauded young man who walked the stage that night.

The Chairman and Chief Executive Officer of The Black Alliance opens the Beautillion from an elevated stage. The message of the Chairman is action-based and often underscores the activities of the organization. It also strongly emphasizes the role of the ball in recognizing excellence and potential within the ranks of African American youth as well as harkening back and taking a bow to strong leaders of the past. These opening words are followed by a prayer. The theme of uplift is emphasized at the beginning of each ball as the audience sings James Weldon Johnson's (1871–1938) 'Lift Every Voice and Sing,' a popular secular hymn. Its theme of advancing black people through democratic ideals and faith have made it a popular inspirational hymn for the American black community:

> Lift every voice and sing
> Till earth and heaven ring.
> Ring with the harmony of liberty;
> Let our rejoicing rise
> High as the listening skies.
> Let us resound loud as the rolling sea.
> Sing a song full of the faith that the dark path has taught us,
> Sing a song full of the hope that the present has brought us.
> Facing the rising sun of our new day begun,
> Let us march on till victory is won.

Following the standing and singing of the Negro National Anthem important guests and members of The Black Alliance are introduced to the audience. Typical important guests can include, but do not always include, elected political officials. The introduction of The Black Alliance members varies from year to year ranging from formal presentation on stage to more informal recognition of members seated in the audience.

Following the introductions is the keynote address. Keynote speakers are inspirational in tone and generally drawn from the ranks of the African American community. Messages I heard from the stage both stressed the reality of statistics indicating tough roads ahead for young black men, but also the importance of keeping faith, focus, and commitment in the face of these harsh realities. In 1996 Reverend Michael Coleman urged the young people in the audience to use their faith to hone character and craft exemplar lives. Those that fall in the face of adversity, the audience was told, may have many excuses, but they are 'choosing something other than iron to sharpen themselves by' (Lynch 1996, as summarized in my notes). Coleman painted a grim picture of many black men's lives but called for the young men of the community to rise above and defy the statistics. As summarized in my notes, 'The statistics say that some are going to die, but lives are not shaped by statistics; they are shaped by the hearts of great people.' In 1998 the speaker was a man that grew up in the community and had gone on to have a successful career as a lawyer. He presented a story of a life influenced by strong black male leadership and mentoring, and perhaps most importantly the strong role of education in uplift.

The keynote addresses delivered each year were in the spirit of Henry Louis Gates's calls for black leadership to acknowledge the despair haunting large percentages of black males in the United States, while at the same time find ways to motivate individuals to work for personal and community uplift and change. Gates stresses that the 'first mission' of black leadership 'isn't the reinforcement of the idea of black America' but rather, to find 'a way of speaking about black poverty that doesn't falsify the reality of black advancement; a way of speaking about black advancement that doesn't distort the enduring realities of black poverty' (1997: 38). Like Gates, the male leaders sponsoring this event are attempting to narrow the gap between the growing black underclass and the advancing middle class. By recognizing excellence within the ranks of black male youth they are attempting to defy statistics and advance young black males into positions of respect and power in American society.

Following a brief intermission the beaux are introduced to the audience. Beaux, like their female counterparts, are presented on a runway to a mostly African American audience. The young men wear matching conventional formal suit styles that add unity and decorum to the event. The uniformity of dress is significant given the African American community's tendency to use dress to mark individual interpretations of black style. The young men walk down the runway as their accomplishments are announced to the audience. At the end of the runway, each young man takes a bow and acknowledges the audience. Although these young men are dressed in a uniform manner, individual style is expressed in gesture and walk and to a limited extent through hairstyles. While some young men have a conventional presentation style, the solo walk down the runway and finale bow are often used by young men as venues for expressing their own personal style. The audience takes visible and audible delight in the young men who play the audience using body movement and gesture.

After acknowledging the audience the young beaux walk back up the runway to meet their female escort. The escort's name is announced as she enters the main stage to be walked down the runway by her male partner. Female escorts are generally African American women from the community and are friends and/or girlfriends of the beaux. Female escorts are also in formal dress styles, but wear a wider range of individually chosen dresses. Typical dresses are black full-length evening gowns that are cut close to the body. They often include a high slit to allow movement and also reveal the leg of the wearer as she walks. Open back midriff styles and bodice cuts that reveal cleavage are common. Paired, the candidate and his escort present an eveningwear appearance that contrasts with the 'wedding-day look' constructed for the young women's debutante ball. The audience and beaux are frankly appreciative of the beauty and sensuality of the young female escorts. In this sense the event harkens back to the black beauty contests and fashion shows that showcased black female beauty earlier in the twentieth century. Following the introduction of the female escort, the couple walks down the runway, acknowledges the audience, and is seated at a head table with attending family members. The young beaux are typically more restrained in gesture and movement during the second walk down the runway, perhaps granting attention to the beauty of their female escorts.

While in most aspects the individual presentation of the beaux is similar to the debutantes, the stage show climaxes with a dramatic show of group identity, the 'Salute to the Beaux,' that has no comparable equivalent within the debutante ritual. The format of the Salute to the Beaux was different all three years I attended. In 1996 Black Alliance members lined up in two columns creating a passageway stretching the length of the runway. The beaux then walked through this path between the two lines of male mentors and were welcomed into the brotherhood of adult men often through physical contact in the form of handshaking and shoulder patting. In the second year, only the young beaux were featured in the Salute. As a group they came to the front of the runway and danced for the audience, taking turns at being center stage, similar to the way jazz musicians alternate between solo and group performance. Tuxedo jackets were typically dramatically thrown over the shoulder as the young men fell into athletic shows of dancing ability and personal pride. In 1998, the beaux formed a long line up the center of the runway and displayed personal style through dance, gesture, and eye contact.

The Salute reminded me of the dramatic shows of group pride and cohesiveness that characterize the bonding rituals displayed by many largely black member basketball teams prior to basketball games. An energy is released as the presentation styles of the young men play off each other on stage to the rousing theme by Black Men United. The lyrics of the BMU song express the coming-of-age theme as well as the importance of holding on to dreams and standing tall:

You Will Know
Um, Um, Um, Um
Yeah, Yeah
When i was a young boy
I had visions of fame
They were wild and they were free
They were blessed with my name

And i grew older
And i saw what's to see
That the world is full of pain
That's when i picked up the pieces
And i regained my name

And i fought hard ya'll
To cover my place
And if right now you could ask me
And it all seems in place

Chorus:
Your dreams ain't easy
Just stick by young man
You must go from boys to men
You must act like a man
When it gets hard ya'll
You must grab what you know
Stand up tall and don't you fall
You will know (*4 times*)

And i know your crying
Cause it's all in his fate
And the things you want you can't have
It just all went away

But life ain't over
Ohh . . .
Just grab the wind
And make the mends
And the vow will take you far

Following the Salute to the Beaux special and lifetime awards are presented to male leaders from the community. Similar to the Cotillion Ball, the stage events close with the beaux leading their female escorts to the dance floor for a formal waltz. The informal dance with music provided by the disc jockey closes the night.

The dress, appearance, and modes of self-presentation of these young beaux expresses a synthesis of West African and American aesthetics that has a long American history dating back to the slavery period. Four themes emerged as significant as I related what I observed at the Beautillion Ball to the history of African American male dress and appearance styles: (1) movement as an expression of style, (2) importance of wearing a 'smart' suit, (3) having a hat, having a 'do', (4) importance of street style.

Background and History: Style and Movement

Male escorts at the Cotillion and candidates at the Beautillion often use their walk and gestures to express distinct versions of male style that draw enthusiastic responses from the audience. In contrast to the female debutantes, who work hard to conform to conventional styles of formal presentation, males at both balls openly play with and challenge convention through confident displays of stylized movement and gestures. Young men with the most distinct styles of self-presentation are clearly appreciated by the audience, and clearly gain confidence through the movement of their bodies on stage.

Recognition of black men's distinct styles of movement and gesture have been noted by observers since the day black slaves landed on the American coastline. In a different form, but working out of a shared body of West African aesthetic principles, black men, like black women, used creativity and spirit to compose an artistic response to imposed standards of dress and behavior. The medium for women was textiles and clothing, the medium for men included the body itself. The result was a long history of integrating West African and American forms of movement and gesture into a distinct self-presentation style that has echoes and impact beyond the confines of the African American community.

Robert Farris Thompson's research on dance and movement in West Africa using internal sources to uncover the criteria used to judge and the principles governing body movement revealed distinct and significant contrasts with Euro-American attitudes. Drawing attention to the self through conscious use of distinct styles of movement and gesture is central, argued Thompson, to West African ideals of self-presentation. A thirty-year-old male from the Dan population in Northeast Liberia stated that among his people it is important for him to 'move with flair [and add] something to my dance or walking, to show my beauty to attract the attention of all those around me, even if they are thinking of something else' (Thompson 1974: 16). In the interview this man goes on to stress the importance of bodily movement as a key component of the aesthetic evaluation of a person:

> Dan can criticize a handsome person by the way he walks and the way he acts even though this person is otherwise completely beautiful . . . There is no mistaking a completely beautiful person who walks and talks and acts and looks beautifully. We teach the composing of the face, the right way of walking, the right proportion of standing, the right way of acting with the body when making conversation (Thompson 1974: 251)

Gender-based differences in preferred modes of walking are noted in Sylvia Boone's research among the Mende of Sierre Leone. According to Mende aesthetic canons women's carriage should be smoother and more majestic, contrasting with a male style stressing assertive energetic movement (1986: 126). These differences in body deportment translate into the aesthetic underlying West African male dance styles that emphasize 'vital movement' of distinct parts of the body:

> The concept of vital aliveness leads to the interpretation of the parts of the body as independent instruments of percussive force. It is not usually permissable to allow the arms to lapse into an absent-minded swaying while the legs are stamping fiercely. The dancer must impart equal autonomy, to every dancing portion of this frame. (Thompson 1974: 9)

Male dancers capable of bold, dramatic movements that draw the attention of the audience are the most heavily lauded among the Dan: 'Shyness in Dan dance is bad; shyness in dancing spoils the effect of the art; a good dancer must be bold' (Thompson 1974: 252).

Early responses to the carriage and deportment styles of black African slaves indicate that differences between deportment styles of male and female slaves existed. While women described in runaway slave advertisements are frequently described as being 'proud' in terms of walking style, males are more frequently described as having 'bold,' 'lofty,' 'swaggering,' and 'strutting' styles of deportment (see descriptions in White and White 1998: 72). Black male slaves, robbed of other forms of resistance, turned to their bodies as modes of expression.

As freed black slaves turned to the street as a venue for self-presentation, black men cultivated a street style highly dependent upon movement as a means of personal distinction. African American parades were started in northern cities in the early 1800s and became arenas for self-presentation as well. The parades spread to the South and have some of the same character as the masking rituals I observed in Nigeria in 1995 in that individuals played specific roles that were expressed both in movement and dress. By the early twentieth century New Orleans had become a center of black music with jazz funerals an important venue for expressing black consciousness through sound and movement. Parade marshals of the early jazz funeral parades were marked not only by distinctive dress, but by strong improvisational movements that surprised and delighted the audience. In Shane and Graham White's (1998) book on style they quote jazz musician Sidney Bechet's description of the parade marshals in the parades he attended as a child:

> 'And all those fancy steps he'd have,' Bechet elaborated, 'oh, that was really something! – ways he'd have of turning around himself. People, they got a whole lot of pleasure out of just watching him, hearing the music and seeing him strut and other members of the club coming behind him, strutting and marching, some riding on horses but getting down to march a while, gallivanting there in real style' (141).

Improvisational movement, the ability to use the body to cajole and court the audience through spontaneous and often unpredictable response to the crowd and music, was an important dimension of the performance of the marshal. Bechet, quoted by White and White (1998), continues:

> When the Grand Marshal reached a street corner, 'He'd have a way of tricking his knee, of turning all around, prancing – he'd fool you. You wouldn't be knowing if he was going left or right . . . And that was a big part of it – him stepping and twisting and having you guessing all along. The way he could move, that was doing something for you. He led it.' (141)

The use of stylized movement to confirm and validate black identity continues to be important to African American men throughout the twentieth century. During an historical period when many black men continue to be blocked from obtaining respected professional positions, public presentation of the body is a means of asserting pride in the self and in African American identity. Benjamin G. Cooke, a black drummer, published an article in the 1970s showing the role of kinesic interaction in black culture. Within his article he identifies distinct walking and stance styles of African American males, arguing that 'Just as clothes and hair consciously affirm black people's strength and unity of purpose for the achievement of control of their lives and destinies, so do the selected kinesic forms of nonverbal communication' (1972: 64). He argues that black male walking styles were consciously performed to attract attention and were more rhythmical and sensual than the walks of other American men. The very fact that he was able to identify distinct and named styles of walk[1] and stance among black men indicates the importance granted to body and movement in the community.[2] As the black underclass has grown in the United States, rap culture, including distinct styles of movement, have grown in expressive strength and salience (Kelley 1994), it isn't just the style of clothes you wear, but how you move in them.

The Wearing of a Smart Suit

Movement, as the free means of attaining style, perhaps came first in America, but soon after came the ability to combine and wear American-style menswear with a distinct African American flair. Bricolage, the ability to creatively

1. Styles of walking described by Cooke included chicken walk, Slu Foot or 'down home' walk, soul walk, and pimp walk.
2. While Cooke was able to describe the basic walking styles of black women, their styles of movement were not given distinct names within the community and were not granted the same level of importance.

combine dress elements drawn from a wide cultural palate, was characteristic of West African ensembles and became emblematic of a distinct African American style. It was early observed that black slaves put together ensembles that combined various items of dress in what appeared to their white owners as unorthodox and jarring ways (White and White 1998: 31). The incorporation of elite elements of dress into more common ensembles was in part 'making do' with the clothing that came their way, through exchange with other slaves, or as rewards from their owners. But perhaps more importantly it was an openness to integrating outside cultural influences into aesthetic expression that came with blacks from West Africa. It also arose as a response to the limited range of expression allowed to black male slaves. By creating a stylish presence in the face of adversity black males challenged the position they were assigned in America, and began to create a positive individual and collective consciousness.

The dress of freed Northern black males in the 1800s is described as more dashing and exaggerated than their white counterparts. A tendency to push a fashion trend to the extreme emerged during this period and continues to be a staple element of black style. In the early 1800s men's formal coats were cut open in the chest area, but a Swedish visitor describes black men's coats as being cut 'so open that the shirt sticks out under the arm-pits' (White and White 1998: 94). Hats worn at a jauntier and more rakish angle and accessories that demanded attention were also noted elements in the dress of this early period. The same Swedish visitor goes on to say, 'The waistcoats are of all colours of the rainbow; the hat is carelessly put on one side; the gloves are yellow, and every sable dandy carries a smart cane' (White and White 1998: 94). To be noted, in all cases the modifications to standard menswear styles of the period serve to draw attention to the wearer and create a more demanding and dramatic presentation.

The perceived relationship between sartorial and kinesthetic excess and black male identity was so pronounced that by the end of the 1800s etiquette manuals directed toward black men directed them to tone down their walks and clothing in order to better fit upper- and middle-class models of American masculinity. Despite this published advice a rich culture of black street style continued to develop during this period that was characterized by what the *New York Times* described as 'exaggerated styles and bright hues' (White and White 1998: 245). By 1931 black cultural centers such as Harlem were written up in the newspapers as centers of fashion leadership[3] and the

---

3. White and White (1998) quote the *New York Times*, ' It is said of Harlem that its fashion plates are several jumps ahead of the rest of the world' (1998: 245).

style of African American males began to affect dress styles of the fashion mainstream.

The zoot suit of the 1940s encapsulated the aesthetic preference for over-stated and exaggerated style that characterized black male dress dating back to the slavery period. The entire look of a man wearing a zoot suit demanded attention. The jackets were cut long, the pants were dramatically baggy at the knee and pegged at the ankle, the hats and shoes were wide and flat, and the ties and collar extreme. It was the apparel donned by the most hip. Jazz musicians and young men with hot street style wore the zoot suit out to do their antics. The style was picked up by fashion-conscious youth as a symbol of rebellion in cities throughout the United States and was also worn in Paris (White and White 1998: 261). Kobena Mercer (1990) points out that by the 1940s the less extreme versions of the zoot suit style had entered the fashion mainstream. When viewed in retrospect, the zoot suit moved African American male style into a position of fashion leadership and related black dress styles to popular music.

As black music continued to build a popular audience in the United States, black male style continued to influence overall American fashion trends. Ethnic dress of the 1960s and 1970s, disco fashions of the 1980s, and hip hop styles of the 1990s all emerged out of the interplay between music and fashion, all heavily influenced by African American expressive culture. The aesthetic preference for strong bold presentation, carried over from the slavery period, is still a mainstay of contemporary black male hip hop fashions that rely heavily on over-sized baggy pants combined with regalia drawn from the world of sports such as starter jackets. Even more so than zoot suit fashions, hip hop influences the dress of broad sectors of American male and female youth, challenging the labeling of black culture as 'marginal' and granting black male style a formative role in American popular culture.

Stylistic excess and drama expressed through apparel choices are largely held in check by the prescribed dress codes followed by the participants. The organizers' clear intent is to impose a dress code that encourages the audience as well as the participants to interpret these young men as capable of infusion into the American mainstream. However, the decision to create a 'high style' formal event like the Gentlemen's Beautillion Ball to showcase exemplar young men from the community is in keeping with the reviewed historical emphasis on dramatic public shows of male accomplishment. The importance granted to styles of public presentation, and the pointed creation of a 'Salute to the Beaux' to afford each young man a time to 'strut his stuff' is in character with the black community's history of using smart suit styles and movement as a means of self-validation among men.

The Politics of the Head: Coiffure and Hat Styles of Black Men

The fusion of politics and hairstyles for black men date back to the slavery period. While slaves hair was sometimes shaved or cut as a form of punishment, generally styling the hair was a mode of self-expression allowed by the slavery system. Coiffures thus became a means of self-identification in the slave community. The West African tradition of devoting time to the styling of the hair among men thus continued in America, with evidence of distinct hairstyles captured in descriptions of runaway slaves published in newspapers of the period (White and White 1998: 41). Styles created by African American slaves combined aspects of traditional West African coiffures with popular wig styles worn by white males during the period (White and White 1998: 51). The result was another example of African American style emerging out of the creative ability to bring together African and Euro-American influences into a unique presentation. The showiness of terminating the head with a hat appealed to black men even during the slavery period as White and White (1998) cite evidence that men found ways of fashioning hats from scraps and hand-me-downs.

Following the more general trends of African American male fashion history, the trend toward exaggerated coiffures and dramatic hat styles builds in the late nineteenth and early twentieth centuries and culminates in the 1940s zoot suit trend. The conk hairstyle that went with the zoot suit was as extreme as the clothes it topped. It was a modern dyed look, red artificial coloring defied the natural color of black men's hair and announced modernity and cultural distinctness to a not-quite-ready American public. The style of the conk required a lengthy straightening process but Kobena Mercer is emphatic in arguing that the net result was far from a simple 'copying' of white men's coiffure, but rather a neo-African aesthetic expression demanding recognition and reaction:

> The conk involved a violent technology of straightening, but this was only the initial stage in a process of creolizing stylization. The various waves, curls and lengths introduced by practical styling served to differentiate the conk from the conventional white hair-styles of the day. Rather, the element of straightening suggested resemblance to white people's hair, but the nuances, inflections, and accentuations introduced by artificial mean of stylization emphasized difference. In this way the political economy of the conk rested on its ambiguity, the way it 'played' with the given outline shapes of convention only to 'disturb' the norm and hence invite a 'double-take' demanding that you look twice. (1990: 259)

Topped with the overly wide zoot suit hat the 'double-take' effect was magnified. The zoot suit look was intended to stop and disturb the gaze of

America, and its success was paid testimony by the public reaction to the style which was dramatic and sometimes violent.[4]

For the remainder of the twentieth century black men used their hat and hat styles to craft visually demanding images of themselves with references to modernity and to their West African roots. The range of elements are drawn from many cultures and recombined into a post-modern amalgamation of what it means to be an African American male. Afros, cane-rows, dread-locks, kente cloth hats, stocking caps, fedoras; all worn with a distinct style that draws attention and remarks.

I never observed hats being worn by the young men participating in the Beautillion Balls but barbershops in Waterloo have opened to serve a young black male clientele who want patterns shaved into their hairstyles with a razor and electric clippers. These dramatic haircuts are often worn on the runway by young men who also have created distinct walking and movement styles that set them apart from the mainstream. A recent *New York Times* article described the status of Casper, an established barber serving a hip African American clientele:

> His name is on the lips of the hip-hop set in Sunset Park. The teenagers in baggy pants and Michelin Man jackets up and down Fourth Avenue in Brooklyn know Pedro Quinones, though not as Pedro Quinones. They know him as Casper, the sultan of the shape-up, the master of the Number One Fade, the quick answer to the bad hair day. (Yardley 1999)

While the Waterloo black community is far from New York, young black men express linkages to hip urban style through barbers that carve the latest patterns into their hairstyles which they strut down the runway to an appreciative audience.

The Gentlemen's Beautillion Ball: Interpretive Analysis

On the surface the Gentlemen's Beautillion Ball appears to be a very simple ritual presentation of young black men reconstructed according to models of normative American success. The dictated dress code is uniform and conventional and the message to the young men that education is the key to success is a mainstream American myth. On a deeper level, however, the

4. The Zoot suit fashion caused riots in Los Angeles, Detroit, and Harlem in 1943 as groups of armed servicemen attacked men wearing zoot suits which were popularly interpreted as thumbing their nose at the war effort and patriotism as well as newly instituted rationing regulations (White and White 1998: 249).

ritual is more conflict laden and spirited. Yes, the young men dress in uniform and conventional male style linked in America to versions of institutionalized power, but within individual walks, gestures and hairstyles distinct expressions of African American aesthetics of movement and art emerge.

Cornel West argues that black Americans have crafted strategies of survival and triumph from a selection of Euro-American and West African traditions. Validation and recognition, both key elements in this coming-of-age ritual for young black men, are highlighted by West in the following discussion of black Americans' struggle for identity:

> White supremacist assaults on Black intelligence, ability, beauty, and character required persistent Black efforts to hold self-doubt, self-contempt and even self-hatred at bay. Selective appropriation, incorporation and re-articulation of European ideologies, cultures and institutions alongside an African heritage – a heritage more or less confined to linguistic innovation in rhetorical practices, stylizations of the body in forms of occupying an alien social space (hair styles, ways of walking, standing, hand expressions, talking) and means of constituting and sustaining comradery and community (e.g. antiphonal, call-and-response styles, rhythmic repetition, risk-ridden syncopation in spectacular modes in musical and rhetorical expressions) – were some of the strategies employed. (1990: 27)

While the Beautillion ball rises out of a formal dance tradition in Europe and the United States, as an institution it has been selected and reinterpreted by black Americans as a strategy for validating young black men as they enter into young adulthood.

The Beautillion Ball is an illustration of West's argument, as African American heritage infuses the Beautillion with an energy emanating out of pride and connection to black history and culture. Body movements, gestures, playing with the expectations of the audience, call and response used within the Salute to the Beaux, are all important connections to West African aesthetics and culture that are important components of the Beautillion and Cotillion Balls. While audience members are clearly proud of the academic, community, and athletic records of the young men presented at the Beautillion, it is the gestures, the movements, the style of comradeship expressed during the Salute to the Beaux that draws the most spirited rounds of applause and visible delight. These communal expressions of shared African American heritage and values validate not only the young men on stage but the community overall.

The models of ritual that I have used to frame my research stress the formative and communal aspects of performed ceremonies. Coming-of-age ceremonies therefore not only reflect cultural expectations for young men and women but help to formulate them. Key to the formative role of ritual in constructing gender is the expression of conflicts related to definitions of adult success. While certainly higher education and career-based success are stressed within the Beautillion Ball, there is also a counter-hegemonic model of masculinity that is expressed at the ball that validates young men based upon a different set of criteria. Being true to heritage, connected to the community, alive both in terms of spirituality and aesthetic consciousness are values expressed during the ritual that create a different model of masculinity with roots in African American and West African culture.

Dress and presentation at the African American balls I attended was both a neo-African aesthetic expression as well as a self-conscious effort toward reconstruction following in the footsteps of W.E.B. Du Bois. Clearly the organizers of the two balls deliberately established codes of dress and behavior that created conventional images of men and women that exemplify attitudes and attributes that help to establish the potential and credibility of the young female and male participants. But at the same time, the young men and women bring an aesthetic and spiritual consciousness into the event that is deeply rooted in their cultural heritage.

Clifford Geertz and Victor Turner both argue that ritual emerges in part as a result of cultural conflict. My research on African American male and female coming-of-age balls revealed that versions of black style as well as conscious efforts toward reconstruction combined within these rituals to help individuals and the community struggle to express and resolve problems of growing up in the last decade of the twentieth century as young African American men and women. The male and female coming-of-age balls that are sponsored by adults in the community are effective springboards for the young participants, launching them with confidence into positions within the world and within their communities.

8

Coming of Age in America: Common Threads

Picture to yourself . . . a society which comprises all the nations of the world – English, French, German: people differing from one another in language, in beliefs, in opinions; in a word a society possessing no roots, no memories, no prejudices, no routine, no common ideas, no national character . . . What is the connecting link between these so different elements? How are they welded into one people?

– Alexis de Tocqueville

Being an American is not something to be inherited so much as something to be achieved.

– Perry Miller

As a graduate student enrolled in a research seminar on ethnicity I first read Werner Sollars' (1986) *Beyond Ethnicity: Consent and Descent in American Culture*. It is to the themes captured in the quotations opening his book that I return as I write my concluding words. The two quotations are reprinted above, one a classic reflection on American culture from French observer Alexis de Toqueville and the second an insight from noted American literature scholar Perry Miller. Perhaps out of a selfish desire on my own part to find unity in America, I feel drawn to trying to find the common threads that link the coming-of-age rituals I observed in the Hmong American and African American communities. What is distinctly American, I asked myself, about the appearance, styles and dress these young people constructed to symbolize their coming-of-age in the United States?

Coming of age in America, in the two populations among whom I worked, involved coming to terms with the dominant ideology of the American dream of success. Hochschild (1995), in her analysis of the major tenets underlying American definitions of success quotes a 1993 speech of Bill Clinton: 'The American dream that we were all raised on is a simple but powerful one – if you work hard and play by the rules you should be able to go as far as your God given ability will take you' (15). The young adults I worked with believed in this American dream. They had a fundamental faith in the possibility of achieving success through hard work, education and moral living. An optimism characterized their attitudes despite statistics in both populations indicating that the American dream of affluence and education would be difficult for them to achieve. These attitudes are made visible in the clothing they choose to wear to mark their entrance into adulthood. While in both cases they are decentered populations, they present themselves as capable of achieving success as defined on their own terms.

The two interpretations focused upon how individuals and communities suffering cultural relocation and discrimination use dress to transform and/ or reconstruct male and female gender in order to keep step with changing realities and revise racist and sexist stereotypes. Everyday dress was not treated within this volume. This book is about how dress worn at rites of passage to adulthood, is used to consciously construct versions of male and female gender. Within Hmong and African American communities the redefining of gender by young people on the cusp of entering full status as men and women becomes a means of attaining greater power and respect in American society. As young people dress to fit notions of success for men and women they help define who they are in relation to wider American society. As they struggle to move into respected rather than compromised positions in American society they use dress as a visual emblem underscoring their potential and the promise of their futures.

The notion of achieved success, achieved identity, made reference to by Miller above, is integral to the American dream ideology embraced so widely across the United States. As Americans we pride ourselves upon constructing rather than inheriting our identity. So it is perhaps not surprising that what I found in these American rites of passage to adulthood was not an attempt to re-enact the past, but rather a use of heritage as a response to current realities. So while these young people are clearly proud of their cultural roots, they are interested in achieving their own versions of success. Much of the conflict expressed in the rituals is tied to balancing their cultural inheritance with commitments to modernity and self-invention.

Closing Thoughts: Gender, Ritual, and Dress

A key contribution of this book rests in the dovetailing of notions of ritual as formative with the existing literature on gender, dress and the body. A major contribution also rests in its focus on the role of dress in the cultural construction of gender. The political discourse and research on gender has to date focused primarily on the body. The fact that much of the scholarship has been done by feminists has tended to sway the theoretical development and case studies in the direction of women's bodies and female gender constructions. Working from a political vantage point studies have revealed the self-imposed damage of anorexia nervosa and bulimia (Bordo 1988, 1989, 1993), Victorian concepts of femininity and female health (Groneman 1995), and contemporary concepts of the feminine body (Urla and Swedlund 1995). This volume, while building on the research focused on the body, examines the role of dress in the construction and reconstruction of gender and offers a balanced examination of the impact of cultural constructions of gender on both men and women.

The concept of ritual as an arena wherein conflict is expressed and debated (Turner 1988) is integral to an understanding of these rites of passage. The key conflict expressed in the coming-of-age balls and ball-toss courtship ritual is embed within the relationship of the participants to the American Dream and the dominant ideology of achieving American identity. The statistics are against these young people, yet they and their communities believe in their ability to transcend the economic and social limitations imposed by their status in American society. Dress and appearance styles give these young people and their communities agency, power of expression that allows the spirit to soar and potential to be announced despite the odds, despite the realities of many Hmong and African American lives.

Fundamental differences between dress and appearance styles worn during the rites of passage within the two communities exist. Hmong Americans have newly arrived in the United States and are in the process of transforming their cultural patterns to better fit the American context. *Invention* of dress styles that express debates surrounding gender roles and identity are most important to these young people and their community. In marked contrast, African American participants and their adult sponsors are *reconstructing* gender identity through dress and style. They are challenging the past, rather than inventing the present.

The result is a strong contrast between the forms of dress worn to the coming-of-age ceremonies in the two communities. The newly emergent Hmong American styles of traditional dress are dynamic, creative in their fusion of Hmong and American aesthetic and material culture influences. Similar to the early dress worn by slaves newly arrived from West Africa, Hmong Americans are still in the process of using patterns and techniques of the past to create vital dress styles related to both America and to their past in Laos and China. In contrast, West African influences have worked their way into the American mainstream through the expressive culture of black Americans. What is important to African Americans coming of age in America is to express already formulated versions of African American identity, while at the same time constructing an effective challenge to historical depictions and stereotypes that continue to have an impact on black lives in the United States.

In the coming-of-age rituals in the Hmong American and African American communities in which I worked dress functions as a symbol fusing *models of* everyday reality with *models for* transcendent or idealized reality (Geertz 1973). At the same time that these young people are expressing connections to the real problems and issues of their lives through dress they are also expressing hopes for redefining themselves in more effective ways in American culture. The reflection and debate that I witnessed both within and from participants and audience members was the result of the juxtaposition of the idealized and the normative which occurs within these rites-of-passage to adulthood. Hmong American and African American youth and the organizers of the events have drawn from both the past cultural history as well as Euro-American dress patterns and institutions to create an arena of validation and recognition. The comparison of the compromises of everyday life for these young people and the roles they dress for within the coming-of-age rituals have the potential to spur these young people toward setting high goals for themselves and their communities.

Bibliography

Abebe, T. (1995). Stepping into new roles: Self-respect, poise get most attention at this cotillion. *Waterloo Courier.*

Alexander, A.L. (1995). She's no lady, She's a nigger: Abuses, stereotypes, and realities from the middle passage to Capitol (and Anita) Hill. In *Race, gender, and power in America: The legacy of the Hill-Thomas hearings,* edited by Anita Faye Hill and Emma Coleman-Jordan, 3–25. New York and Oxford: Oxford University Press.

Baizerman, M. and Hendricks, G. (1988). *A study of Southeast Asian refugee youth in the twin cities of Minneapolis and St. Paul, Minnesota.* Washington D.C.: U.S. Department of Health and Human Services, Family Support Administration, Office of Refugee Resettlement.

Baizerman, S., Eicher, J.B. and Cerney, C. (1993). Eurocentrism in the study of ethnic dress. *Dress* 20:19–32.

Barth, F. (1969). *Ethnic groups and boundaries: The social organization of cultural difference.* Boston: Little Brown.

Belton, D., Ed., (1995). *Speak my name: Black men on masculinity and the American dream.* Boston: Beacon Press.

Bernatzik, H.A. (1970). *Akha and Miao: Problems of applied ethnography in farther India.* New Haven: Human Relations Area Files.

Bishop, K. (1984). *The Hmong of central California: An investigation and analysis of the changing family structure during liminality, acculturation and transistion.* Doctoral Dissertation, University of San Francisco.

Bodnar, J. (1987). *The transplanted.* Bloomington: Indiana University Press.

Boone, S. A. (1986). *Radiance from the water: Ideals of feminine beauty in Mende art.* New Haven and London: Yale University Press.

Bordo, S. (1988). Anorexia nervosa: Psychopathology as the crystallization of culture. In *Feminism and Foucault: Reflections on resistance,* edited by I. Diamond, I. and L. Quinby, 87–118. Boston: Northeastern University Press.

Bordo, S. (1989). The body and reproduction of femininity: A feminist appropriation of Foucault. In *Gender/Body/Knowledge/Feminist reconstructions of being and knowing,* edited by M. Jaggar and S. Bordo, 13–33. New Brunswick and London: Rutgers University Press.

Bordo, S. (1993). *Unbearable weight: feminism, western culture and the body.* Berkeley: University of California Press.

Brake, M. (1985). *Comparative Youth Culture: The sociology of youth cultures and youth subcultures in America.* London and Boston: Routledge and K. Paul.

Bruner, E.M. (1986). Experience and its expressions. In *The anthropology of experience*, edited by V. Turner and E.M. Bruner, 3–32. Urbana and Chicago: University of Illinois Press.

Chapman, M., McDonald, M. and Tonkin, E. (1989). *History and Ethnicity*. London and New York: Routledge.

Club Les Dames. (1997). *Portraits of Loveliness*. Waterloo, Iowa: Club Les Dames.

Cohen, A. (1973). *Urban Ethnicity*. London: Tavistock Publications.

Comaroff, J.L. (1987). Of totemism and ethnicity: Consciousness, practice and signs of inequality. *Ethnos 52*(3&4): 301–23.

Connell, R.W. (1995). *Masculinities*. New York and Berkeley, California: University of California Press.

Cooke, B.G. (1972). Nonverbal communication among Afro-Americans: an initial classification. In *Rappin and stylin' out: Communication in urban black America*, edited by T. Kochman, 32–64. Urbana, Chicago, and London: University of Illinois Press.

Cubbs, J. (1986). Hmong art: Tradition and change. In *Hmong art: Tradition and change*, edited by John Michael Kohler Arts Center, 21–30. Sheboygan, WI: John Michael Kohler Arts Center.

Daly, M.C. (1987). Iria Bo appearance at Kalabari Funerals. *African Arts 21*(1).

Detzner, D. (1990). Unpublished interview data.

Dewhurst, C.K. and MacDowell, M. (1983). *Michigan Hmong Arts*. Publications of the Museum, Michigan State University, Folk Culture Series, 3(2).

Diamond, I. and Quinby, L. (1988). *Feminism and Foucault: Reflections on resistance*. Boston: Northeastern University Press.

Dommen, A. (1971). *Conflict in Laos: The politics of neutralization*, New York: Praeger.

Dunnigan, T. (1982). Processes of identity maintenance in Hmong society. In *The Hmong in transition*, edited by G.L. Hendricks, B.T. Downing, and A.S. Deinard, 41–53. Staten Island, N.Y.: Center for Migration Studies.

Eder, D. and Parker, S. (1987). The Cultural production and reproduction of gender: The effect of extracurricular activities on peer-group culture. *Sociology of Education, 60*: 200–13.

Eicher, J.B., (ed.) (1995). *Dress and ethnicity: Change across space and time*. Oxford and New York: Berg Publishers.

Eicher, J.B. and Roach-Higgins, M.E. (1992). Definition and classification of dress: Implications for analysis of gender roles. In *Dress and Gender: Making and Meaning* edited by R. Barnes and J.B. Eicher. Oxford and New York: Berg Publishers.

Eisenhart, M.A. and Holland, D.C. (1983). Learning gender from peers: The role of peer groups in the cultural transmission of gender. *Human Organization, 42*(4): 321–33.

Epstein, A.L. (1978). *Ethos and identity*. London: Tavistock Publications.

Fausto-Sterling, A. (1995). Gender, race, and nation: The comparative anatomy of 'Hottentot' women in Europe, 1815–1817. In *Deviant Bodies: Critical perspectives on difference in science and popular culture* edited by J. Terry and J. Urla, 19–48. Bloomington and Indianpolis: Indiana University Press.

Finck, J. (1982). Clan leadership in the Hmong community of providence, Rhode Island. In *The Hmong in the West: Observations and reports,* edited by B.T. Downing and D.P. Olney, 21–8. University of Minnesota: Center for Urban and Regional Affairs.

Foster, H.B. (1997). *New raiments of self: African American clothing in the Antebellum South.* London and New York: Berg Publishers.

Foucault, M. (1978). *The history of sexuality,* Volume I. New York: Pantheon.

Franklin, C.W. (1984). Black male-black female conflict: Individually caused and culturally nurtured. *Journal of Black Studies, 15*(2): 139–54.

Frazier, E.F. (1962). *Black bourgeoisie: The rise of a new middle class in the United States.* London: Collier Books.

Gaines, K. (1996). *Uplifting the race: Black leadership, politics, and culture in the twentieth century.* Chapel Hill and London: The University of North Carolina Press.

Gates, H.L. Jr. (1997). *Thirteen ways of looking at a black man.* New York: Random House.

Gates, H.L. and West, C. (1996). *The Future of the race.* New York: Vintage Books.

Gates, H.L. Jr. (1988). The troupe of a new Negro and the reconstruction of the image of the Black. *Representations 24*(Fall 1988): 129–55.

Gatewood, W.B. (1990). *Aristocrats of color: The black elite, 1880–1920.* Bloomington and Indianapolis: Indiana University Press.

Geddes, W.P. 1976. *Migrants of the mountains: The cultural ecology of the Blue Miao of Thailand.* Oxford: Clarendon Press.

Geertz, C. (1973). *The interpretations of culture.* New York: Basic Books.

Giddings, P. (1984). *When and where I enter: The impact of black women on race and sex in America.* New York: Bantam Books.

Gilman, S.L. (1985). Black bodies, white bodies: Toward an iconography of female sexuality in late 19th-century art, medicine, and literature. *Critical inquiry 12:* 204–42.

Glazer, N. and Moynihan, D.P. (1975). *Ethnicity, theory, and experience.* Cambridge, MA: Harvard University Press.

Glick-Schiller, N. and Fouron, G. (1990). Everywhere we go we are in danger: Ti Manno and the emergence of a Haitian transnational identity. *American Ethnologist, 17*(2): 329–46.

Goldstein, B.L. (1986). Resolving sexual assault: Hmong and the American legal system. In *The Hmong in transition,* edited by G L. Hendricks, BT. Downing and A.S. Deinard, 135–43. New York: The Center for Migration Studies.

Greenburg, L.M. (1987). Hmong family structure: An historical and contemporary overview. Unpublished manuscript.

Grimes, R.L. (1982). *Beginnings in ritual studies.* Lanham, MD and London: University Press of America.

Groneman, C. (1995). Nymphomania: The Historical construction of female sexuality. In *Deviant bodies: Critical perspectives on difference in science and popular culture,* edited by J. Terry and J. Urla, 219–50. Bloomington and Indianapolis: Indiana University Press.

Hamilton, J and Hamilton, J.W. (1989). Dress as a reflection and sustainer of social reality: A cross-cultural perspective. *Clothing and Textiles Research Journal, 7*(2): 16–22.

Hammond, R. (1991). Call it Rape. *Twin Cities Reader*, 7–11.

Hazzard-Gordon, K. (1990). *Jockin': The rise of social dance formations in African-American culture*. Philadelphia: Temple University Press.

Haynes, M.T. (1998). *Dressing up debutantes: Pageantry and glitz in Texas*. New York and Oxford: Berg Publishers.

Hochschild, J. L. (1995). *Facing up to the American dream: Race, class, and the soul of the nation*. Princeton, New Jersey: Princeton University Press.

Holland, D.C. and Eisenhart, M A. (1990). *Educated in romance: Women, achievement, and college culture*. Chicago and London: University of Chicago Press.

Howard, A. (1990). Cultural paradigms, history, and the search for identity in Oceania. In *Cultural identity and ethnicity in the Pacific* edited by J. Linnekin and L. Poyer, 259–279). Honolulu: University of Hawaii Press.

Jewell, K.S. (1993). *From Mammy to Miss America and beyond: Cultural images and the shaping of US social policy*. London: Routledge.

Kaiser, S. (1997). *The social psychology of clothing: Symbolic appearances in context*. New York: Fairchild.

Kelley, R.D.G. (1994). *Race rebels: Culture, politics, and the black working class*. New York: The Free Press.

Lane, A.J. (1972). The sun and its shadow: A study of blacks in Iowa. Unpublished manuscript.

Lindbergh, S.M. (1988). *Traditional costumes of Lao Hmong refugees in Montana: A study of cultural continuity and change*. Unpublished master's thesis. University of Montana.

Lynch, A. (1996). Fieldnotes, Gentlemen's Beautillion Ball.

Mallinson, J., Donnelly, N. and Hang, L.(1988). *Hmong batik: A textile technique from Laos*. Seattle, WA: Mallison/Information Services.

Mercer, K.(1990). Black hair/Style politics. In *Out there: Marginalization and contemporary culture* edited by R. Ferguson, M. Gever, T. T. Minh-ha, and C. West, 247–66. New York: The New Museum of Contemporary Art.

Mercer, K. and Julien, I.(1988). Race, sexual politics, and black masculinity: A dossier. In *Male order: Unwrapping masculinity,* edited by R. Chapman and J. Rutherford, 97–164. London: Lawrence and Wishart Limited.

Meyer, R., Lee, C., Lee, D., Lyfoung, N., Thao, P., Vang, P., Yang, C., Yang, G.H., Yang, T., Vang, V., Lee, V., Her, S.T., Vang, P., Lenzin, M. (1991). *Hmong tapestry: Voices from the cloth*, St. Paul, MN: Hmong American Partnership.

Moerman, M. (1964). Ethnic identification in a complex society: Who are the Lue? *American Anthropologist, 67*: 1215–30.

Olney, D.P. (1988). *Age and style of leadership in a Hmong community*. Paper presented at the annual meeting of the American Anthropological Association, Phoenix, Arizona.

Ortner, S. (1978). *Sherpas Through Their Rituals*. Cambridge: Cambridge University Press.

Peterson, S.N. (1990). *From the heart and mind: Creating paj ntaub in the context of community*. Doctoral dissertation, University of Pennsylvania.

Pieterse, J.N. (1992). *White on black: Images of African and blacks in western popular culture*. New Haven and London: Yale University Press.

Quincy, K. (1988). *Hmong: History of a people*. Cheney Washington: Eastern Washington University Press.

Robbins, C. (1997). *The Ravens*, New York: Pocket.

Roosens, E.E. (1989). *Creating ethnicity: The process of ethnogenesis*. Newbury Park: Sage.

Rubin, J., Provenzano, F. and Luria, Z. (1974). The eye of the beholder: Parent's views on sex of newborns. *American Journal of Orthopsychiatry 44*: 512–19.

Sarna, J. (1978). From immigrants to ethnics: Towards a new theory of 'Ethnicization'. *Ethnicity, 5*: 370–8.

Schechner, R. (1977). *Essays on performance theory, 1970–1976*. New York: Drama Book Specialists.

Schein, L. (1986). The Miao in contemporary China: A preliminary overview. In *The Hmong in transition*, edited by G.L. Hendricks, B.T. Downing, and A.S. Deinard, 73–85. Staten Island, NY: Center for Migration Studies of New York.

Schiebinger, L. (1993). *Nature's body: Gender in the making of modern science*. Boston: Beacon.

Schildkrout, E. (1974). Ethnicity and generational differences among urban immigrants in Ghana. In *Urban ethnicity*, edited by A. Cohen, 187–222. London: Tavistock Publications.

Scott, G.M. (1987). The Lao Hmong refugees in San Diego: Their religious Transformation and it's Implications for Geertz's Thesis. *Ethnic Studies Report, 5*(2).

Smalley, W.A. (1986). Stages of Hmong Cultural Adaptation. In *The Hmong in transistion* edited by G.L. Hendricks, B.T. Downing, and A.S. Deinard, 7–22.

Sollars, W. (1986). *Beyond ethnicity: Consent and descent in American culture*. Oxford: Oxford University Press.

Sonsalla, D.R. (1984). *A comparative case study of secondary school programs for Hmong refugee students in the Minneapolis and St. Paul schools*. Doctoral Dissertation, University of Minnesota.

Stone, G. (1965). Appearance and the Self. In *Dress, adornment, and the social order*, edited by M.E. Roach and J.B. Eicher, 216–45. New York: John Wiley and Sons.

Tapp, N. (1988). The reformation of culture: Hmong refugees from Laos. *Journal of Refugee Studies, 1*(1): 20–37.

Thompson, R. (1983). *Flash of the spirit: African and Afro-American art and philosophy*. New York: Random House.

Thompson, R. (1974). *African art in motion: Icon and act*. Los Angeles, Berkeley, and London: University of California Press.

Thompson, R. (1973). Yoruba aesthetic criticism. In *The traditional artist in African societies*, edited by W. D'Azevedo, 19–61. Bloomington, Indiana: University Press.

Tullouch, C. (1993). Rebel without a pause: Black street style and black designers. In *Chic thrills: A fashion reader*, edited by J. Ash and E. Wilson, 84–100. Berkeley and Los Angeles: University of California Press.

Turner, V. (1988). *The anthropology of performance.* New York: PAJ.

Urla, J. and Swedlund, A.C. (1995). The anthropometry of Barbie: Unsettling ideals of the feminine body in popular culture. In *Deviant Bodies*, edited by J. Terry and J. Urla, 277–313. Bloomington and Indianpolis: Indiana University Press.

Vang, B. (1990). Unpublished interview data, University of Minnesota.

Vang, T.F. (1979). The Hmong in Laos. In *An introduction to Indochinese history, culture, language and life*, edited by J. K. Whitmore. Ann Arbor: Center for South and Southeast Asia Studies, University of Michigan.

Van DeBurg, W.L. (1992). *New day in Babylon: The black power movement and American culture, 1965–1975.* Chicago and London: The University of Chicago Press.

Vincent, J. (1974). Brief communications. *Human organization, 33*(4): 375–379.

Wahlman, M.S. (1993). *Signs and symbols: African images in African-American quilts.* New York: Museum of American Folk Art.

Walker-Moffit, W. (1995). *The other side of the Asian American success story.* San Francisco: Jossey-Bass Publishers.

Warren, C.A.B. (1988). *Gender issues in field research.* Newbury Park, CA: Sage.

West, C. (1990). The new cultural politics of difference. In *Out there: Marginalization and contemporary culture* edited by R. Ferguson, M. Gever, T.T. Minh-ha, and C. West, 19–38. New York: The New Museum of Contemporary Art.

White, S. and White, S. (1998). *Stylin': African American expressive culture from its beginnings to the zoot suit.* Ithaca and London: Cornell University Press.

Wiegman, R. (1995). *American anatomies: Theorizing race and gender.* Durham and London: Duke University Press.

Wilson, A. (1995). Foreword. In *Speak my name: Black men on masculinity and the American Dream*, edited by D. Belton, xi–xiii. Boston: Beacon Press.

Wolfe, T. (1970). *Radical chic mau-mauing the flak catchers.* New York: Farrar, Straus, and Giroux.

Yang, D. (1982). Why did the Hmong leave Laos? In *The Hmong in the West*, edited by B.T. Downing and D.P. Olney, 3–18. Minneapolis, MN: University of Minnesota, Center of Urban and Regional Affairs.

Yang, D. (1993). *Hmong at the turning point.* Minneapolis, MN: WorldBridge Associates, Ltd.

Yardley, J. (1999). Building fame for $15 a Head: Young barbers cultivate fierce loyalty of teen-age clients. *New York Times.*

Index